D1577293

X-rated

Other titles by Michael Munn and published by Robson Books

Trevor Howard
Charlton Heston: A Biography
The Hollywood Murder Casebook
Hollywood Rogues
Clint Eastwood: Hollywood's Loner
The Hollywood Connection
Burt Lancaster
Stars at War

X-rated

The Paranormal Experiences of the
Movie Star Greats

MICHAEL MUNN

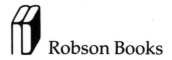
Robson Books

First published in Great Britain in 1996 by Robson Books Ltd, Bolsover House, 5–6 Clipstone Street, London W1P 8LE

British Library Cataloguing in Publication Date
A catalogue record for this title is available from the British Library

ISBN 1 86105 017 8

Typeset in Jansen Text by The Harrington Consultancy
Printed and bound in Great Britain by
Butler & Tanner Ltd, London and Frome

For Will, Elaine and Hannah
– not forgetting their friendly ghost, their Grey Boy
and the White Lady

Contents

Foreword

All over the world, reports keep coming in about UFOs, about hauntings and visions, of psychic phenomena, of the occult, the supernatural, the paranormal.

What exactly are we to make of these occurrences? Who and what are we to believe? The thing is, we keep looking for the truth, and somehow it eludes us. Or most of us. Some believe they have the truth. Shirley Maclaine spent years searching for it. So did Peter Sellers, Whitley Strieber, Peter Cushing, Rudolph Valentino, Glenn Ford and almost everyone else mentioned in this book, including me. But everyone seems to have different answers – some cross over and meet in the middle – and that's what makes the whole subject of the paranormal so fascinating.

Often, a mystery that is solved loses all its fascination. If it was proven once and for all that the Loch Ness Monster did not exist, I feel we would all somehow be hugely disappointed because we gain so much from all the speculation.

Yet the mysteries that concern our very existence – is there life in outer space? Is there life after death? Do we all get reincarnated? – we desperately seek to solve. Perhaps because there just never seem to be absolute answers with tangible, concrete evidence, these mysteries, despite their importance to our well being – for they directly affect our fear of death, and sometimes of life – remain constantly enjoyable and fascinating. But for those who experience the terror of poltergeists or believe they have been abducted by aliens, there is little to enjoy. It is all too real to them, and unfathomably frightening. Yet it is their fear, as well as what they fear, which nevertheless captivates our interest.

There are other factors that maintain our attention. We would like to believe that death is not the end, so we look for reassurance. For many the answers are found in religion and that is a subject which, by and large, I have avoided, for there is not a single devout believer in any faith who does not believe that something miraculous has occurred to them in answer to prayer. Answers to prayer, in fact, seem to be a common occurrence in the lives of the faithful and, in my experience, and with the greatest respect to all believers, even when the request is not heeded, it is gladly accepted as an answer, the explanation being that God did not want what was asked for.

So religious experiences, or those relatively orthodox in nature, have little part in this book. This is the exploration of the paranormal in the world of entertainment, mainly in the cinema but also in television and the theatre since they are all inextricably linked by a common denominator – actors. And writers and directors. What is so curious is that so many of these people have experienced so many different aspects of the paranormal. Although, as will be discussed, there are some definite links between actors and some areas of the supernatural. All will become clear as you read on.

I should explain before you proceed that I never actually went out of my way to collect stories of the supernatural side of showbusiness, since so much of what I was told happened in the natural course of interviewing celebrities during my 20-odd years as a journalist and my on-off career as an actor. I have experienced some of the phenomena that haunt other actors – namely the superstitions that put the fear of god into thespians. I, however, am not superstitious and do not mind going around saying 'Macbeth'. And, having played the part, I know only too well the trepidation which actors face when they take on any role in the Bard's tale of witchcraft, bloody ambition and murder. The curse of Macbeth is a phenomenon that has to be experienced to be believed, and many have.

While some subjects delved into are exclusive to the world of film and theatre, such as *Macbeth*, much of what fills these pages are experiences that happen to people in all walks of life; this book just happens to deal with actors. And that is why I think this book is unique, because a good deal of it will not be found between the covers of other books.

Of course, in writing *X-rated* I have purposely collected more stories but, overall, the whole subject of ghosts and spirits and other spooky things seem to inhabit the world of acting with alarming regularity and I had no problem discovering them. Many of the stories come from interviews I have conducted and from just talking to celebrities I have been associated with in the course of my various careers. So it is not me you have to believe but the likes of Telly Savalas, William Holden, Charlton Heston, Anna Neagle, Linda Hayden, Bette Davis, Kim Novak, Elke Sommer, Arthur C Clarke, Roger Moore, Gloria Swanson, John Hurt, Alan Bates, Jenny Agutter, Peter Sellers and Lynne Frederick, because they told me their tales.

As I have said, I am not superstitious. But I do have an open mind: I found it was important to try to keep my mind open to all possibilities. It is all too easy to ridicule what seems fantastic, although I admit that there are a few times when I found it difficult not to become facetious.

It is impossible to find answers to every paranormal experience, and I do not try to. I do play devil's advocate from time to time and put forward differing views from those who know more about these things I do. You will have to make up your minds about what you read. Of course, if you believe in reincarnation, then your mind is already made up on that subject. If you already believe in extra-terrestrials visiting our Earth and abducting victims, then you will not be persuaded by, say, Arthur C Clarke's arguments.

But, if like me, you have no cut and dried opinions on all or any of the subjects covered herein, you had better be prepared for a few surprises. Above all, keep your mind open.

A Born Again Christian, whose belief and strong faith I admire and respect, told me she has no doubt that, because of what her religion teaches, the paranormal is the work of the Devil –

ghosts, spirits from beyond, UFOs, even hypnosis, are tricks played by Satan to hide the real truth – the Christian truth. But, as I said to her, to take that view is to close your mind to all possibilities.

So read, enjoy, open your mind and remember, the truth is out there. Or so they say.

1

Are You There, Rudy?

There has always been a fascination for the supernatural in the world of the cinema. As, indeed, there has been in the theatre. Actors, it almost seems, are born superstitious. One of the very first lessons an actor learns is how to avoid doing or saying anything that may invoke bad luck. So it is not surprising that so many actors go from being simply superstitious to becoming more aware, often interested, sometimes involved, in the mystical, the supernatural, the paranormal, or whatever description you might care to give that which is unexplainable and mystifying. Something which, in orthodox terms, defies rational explanation.

In Hollywood, during the 1920s and 1930s, the occult was a craze that swept the movie capital. Fortunes were foretold, spirits were raised, ghosts were sought, seances were held. These dabblings in the supernatural were not so much a serious attempt to uncover the mysteries of life and death as they were a mere fad, a trend, something that offered a new way to get high in Hollywood. The occult was actually sweeping the whole of America, but perhaps nowhere in the country was it embraced so enthusiastically as in Hollywood where, wrote Charlie Chaplin in his autobiography, ectoplasm loomed over the city of Los Angeles 'like smog'.

If the occult was enjoying so much success in Hollywood, it had more to do with the fact that this was another forbidden pleasure for film folk to enjoy to excess, like drugs and booze. When these people played, they liked to play harder than that which might be accepted as normal. But that is because they

1

were not ordinary people. They were special, set upon pedestals and heaped with riches and adoration. Many of them believed their own publicity. It must have been hard not to in those days. They were the Golden Days of Cinema.

If it was possible to commune with the dead, then there were Hollywood stars who were going to be the ones to commune. They were the self-styled Chosen Ones of the supernatural. If anyone was going to get results from dabbling in the paranormal in any way whatsoever, then the Chosen Ones of Hollywood would.

Someone once said, 'Seek and you shall find.' And someone else said, 'Be careful what you wish for. You just might get it.' And it's true, because when you go looking for something mystical to happen, you will almost inevitably find it. Fanny Brice did. She was the star of *Ziegfeld's Follies* from 1910 until 1923 and then began a sporadic film career in 1928 with *My Man* followed quickly by *Night Club*. Her life and career was the subject of stage and screen versions of *Funny Girl*, in which she was portrayed by Barbra Streisand and again in the film's sequel *Funny Lady*.

Fanny became fascinated by the supernatural. Like many during the so-called 'Jazz Age' she wanted to see for herself the power of a Hollywood medium – and she saw it. In her excitement, she rushed to tell Charlie Chaplin how spirits were conjured up in an elegant drawing-room, the climax of which was when a table rose from the floor and floated about the room. She died in 1951 at the age of 59, convinced she would soon be contacting this world from the other side. She may well have done so too but, if she has, I have not been able to discover it.

During the earliest days of cinema, it suited the studios to propagate the fascination for the paranormal, so Theda Bara was promoted as the first truly paranormal star. Between 1914 and 1919 she appeared in no fewer than 40 films, notably as *Carmen*, *Cleopatra*, *Madame Du Barry* and *Salome*. On screen she treated servants cruelly, was detestable yet was supposedly irresistible to men and her studio dubbed her The Vamp – short, of course, for vampire. Not that it was suggested she drank the blood of humans, but it was a fitting description of a woman whose very background, said the Fox Studio publicity department, was steeped in mysticism and the occult.

Theda was, they said, 'a crystal-gazing seeress of profoundly occult powers' who was born 'in the shadow of the Sphinx' to an Arabian princess and a European artist – or maybe an Arab sheikh and a European princess, the story varied. Her name, they said, was an anagram of Arab Death. In fact she was born Theodosia Goodman in Cincinnati in 1890.

She wore indigo make-up to accentuate her pale demeanour and she did her best to live up to the image that her studio had saddled her with. She surrounded herself with human skulls, ravens and an assortment of death symbols. When the press were invited to meet her, they entered a room heady with incense, to find her stroking a serpent. 'Nubian slaves', supposedly authentic and imported, waited upon her. She gazed into her crystal ball and predicted that her up-coming films would all be box-office hits. She called upon her powers of prophecy to declare that audiences would love her as long as she remained in Hollywood.

She should have heeded her own premonition. She left Hollywood in 1919 to work on Broadway in New York. She returned in 1925 and made two more films, the last being *Madame Mystery*, a Hal Roach short in which she parodied herself. The more sophisticated movie audiences of the immediate post-First World War era were no longer enchanted by screen vamps. Later, languishing in obscurity, she was asked if she really had occult powers. She laughed and said, 'If I had, I would have seen it coming.' She died, virtually forgotten, in 1955.

During her brief reign, Theda had made the whole idea of the occult too fascinating to leave alone and a group of Hollywood people of no small repute took to it like ducks to water. Before long they had the occult pretty well exclusively wrapped up for themselves. They were Rudolph Valentino, Natacha Rambova,

Nazimova and June Mathis. As a group they practised seances, astrology and discussed reincarnation.

There was nothing to suggest that Valentino would become such a purveyor of the supernatural when he was born as Rodolfo Alfonzo Raffaele Pierre Philibert Guglielmi to good Catholic parents in Castellaneta, Italy, in 1895. His father, an army vet, sent 13-year-old Rodolfo to a military academy but the recruit failed to make an officer. He was later turned down by a naval academy and drifted to Paris in search of a life. He begged on the streets but managed to make his way to New York in 1913 where he drove taxis on Broadway, and had an assortment of other occupations including petty theft.

Then he took to demonstrating his dance skills in dance halls and night clubs, making a success as a gigolo. But he got into trouble with the law again and ended up in a notorious detention centre known as the Tombs.

By this time he had come to the attention of Russian dancer and actress Alla Nazimova who had just begun a glittering film career. She managed to get him released and then helped him on his way to Hollywood in 1917 where he landed small roles in films, usually playing exotic dancers or greasy villains.

In 1920 Nazimova introduced him to one of her protégés, Jean Acker; he married her. Much later she accused him of failing to satisfy her sexually. It turned out their marriage was never consummated, due to the fact that Acker, like Nazimova, was a lesbian. Acker was not to remain long a part of Valentino's life, for the fates had someone else waiting in the wings for Rudy. She was the supernatural-powered Natacha Rambova.

But before that happened, influential screen writer June Mathis helped him to land the starring role in *The Four Horsemen of the Apocalypse* in 1921; that picture made him a star. That same year he starred with Nazimova in *Camille*, and it was on the set of that film that Nazimova introduced him to Natacha Rambova.

In reality Rambova was American heiress Winifred Hudnut, a dancer from Salt Lake City trying to make a name for herself in Hollywood. In trying to make that name, she changed it to something that sounded suitably Russian, hence Natacha Rambova, and set about building a successful career as a film art director. With her psychic powers, she became the centre of the group in their endeavours to contact the other side.

Like Acker, Rambova was a protégé of Nazimova – and a lesbian. Or at least, she liked men and women. Valentino fell in love with her and married her, but all too soon since it turned out he had not legally divorced Acker. He had not understood that a full year between divorce and remarriage was required by Californian law, and he was charged with bigamy.

Curiously, Valentino and Rambova began their married life – albeit a bigamous one – living in a house on Sunset Boulevard with a third party, cameraman Paul Ivano. Rambova began handling all of Valentino's business interests, but her complete lack of tact and bombastic manner caused trouble between him and his studio, Famous Players-Lasky, later to become Paramount.

In 1921 he became the ultimate heart throb of women all around the world as *The Sheik*. It was said that women fainted in the cinemas. He was soon influenced by Rambova's psychic nature and he began to receive spiritual messages of his own. His business manager, S George Ullman, said that Valentino was not superstitious 'in any small and trivial way', telling Kevin Brownlow that Rudy 'had no objection to spilling salt, walking under a ladder – these things he ridiculed. The psychic never became a religion to him, but he yielded to its influence more than to any form.'

During a seance, an Indian spirit called Black Feather made his presence known to the group and announced he was Valentino's spirit guide. Rudy was to consult Black Feather before making any important decisions. So when Rambova insisted that he quit the studio, he could cite Black Feather as being the influence behind his decision; a decision which Famous Players-Lasky viewed with dismay. They reminded him that he had a contract with them and forbade him from making films for any other studio.

Rather than be dictated to, Valentino did not make a film for two years while he and Rambova embarked on an extensive personal dance tour. It was, the spirits told Rambova, the way forward. So forward they went, across the United States and holidaying in Europe.

When they returned to Hollywood, they reached a compromise with their studio and Valentino was allowed to work for an independent producer, J D Williams, on *Monsieur Beaucaire*. Rambova was art director on the film and turned up on the set from time to time to deliver messages from the spirits as to how Valentino should play his part. It has to be said that critics raved about his performance so possibly the spirits knew what they were talking about. But audiences did not respond to the film. Under Rambova's influence, he had come across as an effeminate character, and women, the majority of his audience, disapproved.

When his contract with Paramount came to an end, he and Rambova set up their first independent production, Cobra. Rambova herself wrote the screenplay, working on it while the film was being shot and delivering newly typed pages each morning. At night she put herself into a trance and wrote what her spirits told her to write. According to Colleen Moore, who was making a film at the same studio, Rambova produced great rolls of illegible script, and so June Mathis was brought in to finish the job.

Mathis often joined Valentino, Rambova and Nazimova in paranormal evenings. But there is no evidence to suggest that Mathis used any influence other than her own talent as a script writer. Rambova was said to go into sudden trances on the studio sets and utter words that meant nothing to anyone in particular. But no one laughed in Valentino's presence. She went on planning his life, guided by the spirits, and he allowed her to get on with it. But under her influence, his image became more and more effeminate. Yet there is no evidence that he was, as some have suggested, a homosexual. To put matters right, Valentino made *The Son of the Sheik* in 1926. It was the last film he ever made.

Valentino always said that when he eventually died, he would find a way of coming back, perhaps in a reincarnated form. But he failed to predict his untimely death on 23 August 1926, from peritonitis.

Curiously, someone did have a premonition of his death but it was not one of the group. It was silent screen queen Gloria Swanson. Before Rambova came into Valentino's life, Swanson had been one of his closest friends. She insisted that they were never romantically linked, but as good friends they often went horse riding together. One day he presented her with a gift – a riding crop with her monogram on the silver handle.

Five years later, she was riding a horse at a country club in Pinehurst in North Carolina, practising for a new film in which she had a number of riding scenes, when she suddenly became alarmed. She felt that she should never ride a horse again, and she also felt concerned for Valentino. In her hand was the riding crop he had given her.

She had meant to call him, but didn't. She never rode again and, shortly after the occurrence, Valentino died. She bitterly regretted not calling him, wondering if she could have somehow saved his life.

Valentino, mourned by thousands of women, did manage to make his presence known from beyond the grave. Rambova claimed that she was still in touch with his spirit. In more recent years he may have been paying Glenn Ford the occasional visit. At Ford's Hollywood home, he and his wife Cynthia often heard the echoes of what sounded like a long past party in their garden.

'There is laughter as though someone has just told a joke,' said Cynthia, 'and the clink of glasses. Once when we went downstairs in the morning all the garden furniture had been arranged in a circle. At least it's a happy manifestation. Once I even smelled cologne of a type that isn't made any more – the sort that Valentino wore.'

Not that Valentino has limited his after-life existence to America. In Britain a renowned medium, Leslie Flint, was in touch with him. Flint had seen Valentino in *The Four Horsemen of the Apocalypse* as a boy and was a huge fan. He later joined the Spiritualist Church and began receiving messages from the Church's mediums that he had a spirit helper who was dressed in sheik's robes who was 'an Arab and not an Arab'. This spirit helper instructed Flint to develop his mediumship to serve humanity.

One day he received a letter from a woman in Munich who said that Valentino had come through to her, had given her Flint's name and address, and the instruction that he was to become Valentino's medium. Flint had never met this woman.

Flint was not absolutely sure that he wanted to become a medium. As a member of the Spiritualist Church, he was one day invited to sit in a circle of church members – three men and three women. During the session a message came through from Valentino – the Arab who was not an Arab – and repeated the instruction to Flint to develop his mediumship and serve humanity.

He returned to this circle several times and at one time went into a trance. Through him Rudolph Valentino spoke. Flint was promptly told by the Spiritualists, 'If you develop in our circle, we hope you will contact entities a lot more spiritually evolved than Hollywood actors!'

Presumably not wanting to lose contact with his famous Hollywood spirit, Flint left that group and in time he became a highly respected medium. He claimed that through him many famous people from history have spoken, including Queen Victoria, Robert Browning, Winston Churchill, George Bernard Shaw and Oscar Wilde, who told Flint, 'being dead is a most extraordinary business, especially when you are talking to people on Earth who are supposed to be alive and are very much dull and dim in consequence.'

With so many people inhabiting the other side and in touch with Leslie Flint, Rudolph Valentino was in good company.

2

Ghosts of Stage, Screen and Cemeteries ·

Apparently the chances of seeing a ghost are about one in ten for all of us. Just exactly what ghosts are is open to debate even between those who believe in them. What *is* certain is that their appearance can cause terror to some people, and wonderment to others.

There are two types of ghost. 'Cyclic' ghosts – otherwise known as 'recurring' ghosts – appear annually at specific locations, usually recreating a traumatic event to do with their own deaths. Most other ghosts are known as 'spontaneous' ghosts and they can appear to be as real and as solid as you and I; assuming you, like me, are still of this world. According to the president of the Ghost Club of Britain, Peter Underwood, spontaneous ghosts act naturally and are often only recognized as being ghosts in 'the cold light of day' – or to use a Sam Goldwynism, 'In the cold night of day'.

So the problem with seeing a ghost is that you cannot be absolutely sure that what you saw was a ghost. Which is what happened to Telly Savalas. He told me this tale:

I was on Long Island where a friend of mine lived in a rather remote area. When I left his place it was early morning, still dark, and I remember looking at the car clock and seeing that it was 3 am. Then I saw that the gas tank was just about on empty. I pulled in to a café that was open through the night, had a coffee and asked where the nearest gas station was. This guy said, 'Go out back, take the path through the

9

woods and you'll come to a freeway and you'll find the gas station a couple of miles further on.'

I thanked him and went outside and was about to find my way round to the back when I saw this black Cadillac. The driver called me over. I remember he had a sort of high-pitched voice, and he asked me if I needed a lift. I said, 'Yeah, thanks.' I climbed in next to him and said I needed to get some gas for my car.

He drove me to the freeway, found the gas station, and I went to pull out my wallet to pay for the gas and found it was missing – I'd dropped it, I guess. So this guy loaned me a dollar. I told him to write his name and address down for me so I could pay him back. He wrote his name. I'll never forget it: Harry Agannis.

He drove me back to my car, I filled up and he was gone. I wanted to thank him properly, so the next morning I looked him up in the phone book, found his number and dialled. A woman answered, and I said, 'Would Harry Agannis be your husband?' She said, 'Yes, he was.' I said, 'Could I speak with him please?' She said, 'No, I'm sorry but that's not possible.' I said, 'Why not?' She said, 'Because he's been dead for five years.'

Well, the first thing I felt was total shock. Then I felt really sorry for this poor woman who has me ringing up asking to speak to her long dead husband. Well, that might have been it, but it really played on my mind. I tried to persuade myself that I had made some mistake. But I had the paper which he had written his name and address on. Maybe it was someone playing a cruel practical joke. So a few days later I paid a call on Mrs Agannis and showed her the paper and asked, 'Is this your late husband's handwriting?' She studied it and said, 'No doubt about it. That's his handwriting.'

She asked me what this man claiming to be her husband had been wearing. So I told her about the suit this guy wore, and she said, 'That was the suit we buried him in.' And with that we just sat there looking at each other, saying nothing.

When people say, 'You look like you've seen a ghost,' that's what it was like with that good lady and me. I mean, was it a ghost? I don't know what else you would call it.

Savalas was not, as far as I know, a seeker of the supernatural, and as a former GI who was awarded a Purple Heart in the Second World War, he always seemed to take life as it came at him. He was, he said, a 'good down-to-earth Greek boy from New York,' a 'pussycat on the inside and thick-skinned on the surface'. He did not look for answers in life and readily accepted his fate to play vile villains in films like *The Dirty Dozen*, *On Her Majesty's Secret Service* and *Beau Geste*, figuring there would come a time when someone 'ugly like me will be loved for myself' and not his looks. And, of course, he was right: he became a star in his own right as TV's top cop *Kojak*.

As a man who accepted fate, he never tried to analyse his encounter with his ghost. 'It just happened to me,' he said. 'Why, I don't know. It's not like my life was in danger and he was sent as my guardian angel or whatever. But isn't that what makes the unexplainable so fascinating, because it is unexplainable? Maybe when I've passed on, I'll figure it out.' Telly passed on in January 1994, shortly before his seventieth birthday.

Back in the early 1960s, when Telly Savalas was making a good living at being a major supporting actor, Kim Novak was enjoying her reign as a sex symbol that had begun the previous decade in films like *The Man with the Golden Arm* and *Pal Joey*. But as the public became less enchanted with her style of cool sensuality and the years failed to turn her into a successful character actress, she faded, and then made a welcome return in 1980 in *The Mirror Crack'd*. During her reluctant promotion of the film – I say reluctant because she really did not seem comfortable being interviewed – she told a rather chilling tale of her previous excursion to Britain to make *The Amorous Adventures of Moll Flanders* in 1966.

She recalled that it was filmed at a seventeenth-century house built round the keep of a Norman castle at Chilham in Kent.

'Nobody thought to mention that this old place had a few ghosts,' she said.

She had her own room in the house and was one evening relaxing and playing records, putting on a particular favourite that she felt like dancing to. Although she was gyrating about the room, she suddenly felt cold. She said, 'A powerful force seemed to grab me round the waist. I was lifted off my feet and slammed against the wall.'

There was never any explanation for what occurred, although she suggested, 'Maybe it didn't like pop music'.

Novak seemed very cool about the whole thing, unlike Roger Moore who as TV hero 'the Saint', one of *The Persuaders*, and as James Bond in seven movies, may be considered a pretty fearless man of action. But a ghostly encounter in his own home left him somewhat stirred and shaken. He has never been able to explain quite what took place but this is how he told the story.

One night I was sound asleep when I suddenly woke up. It felt as though someone was in the room. It all sounds rather like something out of a Hammer horror film, but I lay there with the moonlight pouring into the room through the window, and this mist floating across the bed. Yes, a mist, it sounds like a special effect, but that's what it was. I was absolutely petrified and couldn't move until it had gone. I checked my watch and saw that it was 2 am. Apparently that's the normal thing people do when they have such an experience: check the time.

The next night the same thing happened: same time, same sort of mist. The next morning I decided I didn't want to sleep in that room again, but our home help who was a devout Jehovah's Witness, said I should leave the Bible opened at the 23rd Psalm by the side of my bed. I'm not a religious man myself but I decided to give it a try. After all, I didn't want some ghost chasing me out of my own bedroom. So I left the Bible open on the bedside table, and it worked.

Some who have ghosts in their homes learn to live with them, such as Adrienne Posta, the British actress of numerous comedy films like *Here We Go Round the Mulberry Bush*, *Up the Junction* and *Up Pompeii*. She has lived with a ghost in her house for years.

> He's very friendly. The house has such a nice atmosphere I would hate to leave it. Sometimes he gets a bit agitated, then he crashes about and opens and closes doors. That's a nuisance, but not really frightening. The only time I got really annoyed was when he persistently threw open my bedroom door in the middle of the night. I was really beginning to suffer from lack of sleep and felt I had to do something about it. So one night I retaliated. I threw a book towards the door when it opened and gave him a piece of my mind. The pestering stopped.

In his book *Ghosts and How to See Them*, Peter Underwood points out that there is really no need to be frightened if you see a ghost since they rarely hurt people. He says that although sights and sounds may be startling and there may be damage to furniture and other objects, 'it is unlikely anyone has been injured'. But presumably you must remember to duck if pots and pans come flying across the room. It is certainly true that many people who, having realized they have a ghost of their own which proves itself not to be particularly menacing, learn to live with it. That is what happened to actress/singer Suzi Quatro.

Although born in the United States, she made her name as a rock singer in Britain during the 1970s and went on to co-star in the hit TV series *Happy Days*. She has remained based in England, pursuing a successful acting career and enjoying success in the West End revival of *Annie Get Your Gun*. From her proceeds as a rock star she bought her very own haunted mansion.

Hyde Hall in Essex is a Grade II listed, sixteenth-century house with oak-panelled rooms, beamed ceilings, open fireplaces, and at least two ghosts. 'One we call Richard,' said Suzi Quatro, 'lives in the guest room. The other is a little girl.' She does not find the ghosts at all frightening and says of the house, 'As soon as I saw Hyde Hall I knew I had to have it. It has a wonderful atmosphere. It's a child's dream, too, with lots of nooks and crannies.' She lived there for 20 years before deciding to sell it in 1994 when it went on the market for £450,000.

Cilla Black, 1960s British pop singer and 1990s star of TV's *Surprise Surprise* and *Blind Date*, had her own surprise, surprise, when she woke up to find the ghost of a teenage girl standing by her bed. It happened four times in all over a seven-year period. Said Cilla:

When it first happened, in my drowsy state I thought one of the children had come into the bedroom, perhaps wanting a drink of water or upset by a nightmare. The second time, I knew it was a ghost. She was so sweet, I didn't feel frightened. In fact, believe it or not, I quite liked her being there. She appears to be wearing a long dress, like a nightie, and just stands there. She never looks at me.

I have actually spoken to her, asked her why she has come back and why she can't find peace. But she never answers. She just floats away through the door.

An explanation as to why Cilla's ghost ignores her is put forward in a suggestion by Peter Underwood that ghosts are in a different dimension from human beings which is why they are rarely aware of our presence. He also suggests that there is evidence that many ghosts who walk the same routes and appear in the same rooms, do so even when no living person is present.

Stephanie Lawrence, the star of stage musicals like *Evita*, lived as a child in a house that had once been an army training school on Hayling Island, off the south coast of England. It was full of long corridors and was called Stonehenge because, her parents discovered, there was a spot in the garden where a soldier's horse had been buried which had been marked by a pile of stones. But before this was known by the family, young Stephanie had a frightening experience:

One evening I was walking along one of the upstairs corridors when I heard footsteps behind me and what sounded like the patter of dog's paws. I spun round quickly and there was a soldier in bright red and gold uniform with a golden Labrador by his side. I was absolutely terrified and rushed downstairs to find my brother. I've never forgotten it. I can still see him standing there.

It was after that incident that Stephanie's parents began to discover more about the house's past. Various army relics from the time of the Crimean War, such as a scarlet and gold braid uniform, much like the one Stephanie's ghost wore, were found under the floorboards.

Showbusiness-related ghosts are not exclusive to Britain. In Hollywood a number of film and TV stars have experienced hauntings. And some stars have been seen as ghosts.

Charlene Tilton, Lucy Ewing in *Dallas*, lived as a child with her mother and grandfather in a small apartment in Hollywood. Her grandfather looked after her while her mother went out to work but he died when Charlene was six.

Since her mother still had to go out to work, Charlene had to remain in the apartment on her own. One day her mother came home to find her sitting on the doorstep trembling with fright. She explained that there was 'somebody scary' in the apartment. Her mother told her that the spirit of her grandfather was still with them.

As the years went by, strange things happened. Charlene recalled:

I remember very clearly something incredibly scary when I was a teenager. One day a neighbour called in and asked if I would turn down the radio, which was blaring out pop music. In a teenage tantrum I refused.

Then things began to happen. The plug jerked out of the wall without anyone being near it. When I pushed it back into the socket it was jerked out again so violently that sparks flew. The neighbour stood there with her mouth open, struck dumb by what she had seen, but we knew it was the ghost again.

When I left home to live with my boyfriend, I expected to leave the spirit of my grandfather back at my mother's apartment. Our own apartment was cheery and cosy, but after a while my boyfriend complained that it felt spooky. You could sense something or someone invisible when you walked into an empty room. There were pockets of cold air and nearly every night doors would open silently and close again.

I finally moved out in an attempt to escape the ghost, and bought a home of my own in Los Angeles. I think I have left grandfather behind because since then I've had no further happenings.

Hollywood actor Chad Everett, leading man of numerous minor films but star of TV in *The Dakotas*, *Medical Center* and *Centennial*, did a do-it-yourself exorcism on a poltergeist that had been making a nuisance of itself. Everett and his wife, Shelby, had a house on Hollywood Boulevard where the lights flickered on and off, usually when Everett and his wife returned home in the evenings. At first they were not too concerned by their troublesome spirit but, when it began throwing crockery and utensils across the kitchen and tipping over furniture about the house, Chad and Shelby grew tired of it all.

Everett said that he decided to treat the poltergeist like a naughty child. 'One day I just stood in the middle of the kitchen while things were being hurled around, and said firmly, "I think you're a fool to waste so much energy. It is difficult enough to communicate yet here you are wasting your precious energy just frightening us. You're just making yourself miserable. Settle down and don't do it again." And it didn't.'

The presence never left the house but it has caused no further trouble. Said Everett, 'I like to think I gave the poor ghost some good advice'.

Hollywood has its fair share of haunted houses, despite its being such a relatively new town – or suburb, as it really is, being just a part of Los Angeles. But Hollywood has had a pretty sordid existence and a fair amount of blood has been spilt there. In 1993, when Madonna bought the mansion once owned by mobster Bugsy Siegel in the Hollywood Hills, she set about having the place refurbished at enormous cost. She had a fully equipped gym built, installed a state of the art sound system in the nine bedrooms and six bathrooms.

It was not so much a house as a fortress complete with a steel and oak drawbridge-style gate, which was supposed to protect Bugsy Siegel from the FBI and vengeful mobsters out to get the money back loaned to him to build his Flamingo Hotel and Casino in Las Vegas. Siegal also had tunnels built under the fortress in which, it was said, he hid bodies of murder victims. These tunnels were discovered during renovations by Madonna's builders.

Said one of the builders, 'Madonna didn't find out about the tunnels until after she bought the house. She went into one room and freaked out. She found some human-looking bones and became convinced that the place was haunted.'

People who visited the tunnels claimed they could sense a spooky presence. Not taking any chances, Madonna hired an exorcist to cleanse the mansion while she returned to her Miami home to wait for her Hollywood one to be completed and rendered ghost-free.

A haunted home awaited German actress Elke Sommer when she and her writer husband Joe Hyams moved into their Hollywood home after getting married in 1964. Sommer is the blonde, sexy star of *A Shot in the Dark, The Oscar, Deadlier Than the Male* and, less conspicuously, *Carry On Behind*, which she was filming at Pinewood Studios in 1974 when I interviewed her. She said:

> Joe, nor I, had any idea that the house we bought in Beverly Hills was haunted. We went to bed and we heard strange noises coming from the dining room. These were banging noises, thumping. I mean, it really was going bump in the night. At first we thought it was burglars, so we went to investigate and found nothing. The same thing happened the next night, and every night, and always the sounds came from the dining room.
>
> This went on until one night there was this pounding on the door, like someone was thumping it like crazy. Joe got

up and opened the door and no one was there. But there was thick smoke – black smoke – billowing up from downstairs. He rushed downstairs and found the dining room on fire.

We got the fire out, and I consulted a few mediums and they all told me that the ghost in our house had set fire to the dining room as an act of mischief but had then regretted its actions and warned us.

After that, Elke and Joe apparently learned to live with their spooky lodger. So much for ghosts rarely injuring anyone, although to be fair to the ghost in question, he did have the decency to warn Elke and her husband they were about to be burned to death.

Perhaps the most haunted place in the world's movie capital is the Hollywood Memorial Park Cemetery. Among the deceased famous to be seen roaming the grounds is Clifton Webb. He had played a couple of unearthly roles in 1950, as a heavenly voice in *Belles on Their Toes* and an angel in *For Heaven's Sake*.

Around that time Darryl F Zanuck, who ran 20th Century-Fox which had Webb under contract, had a premonition about the actor. This shocked the stockholders, not least because Zanuck was not usually given to psychic experiences, but also because his prediction was that Webb would become one of the great film directors in about ten years. Considering that Webb had never directed a film up to that point, it was a rather startling prophecy. If Zanuck had predicted that Webb would stop acting in about ten years and leave it at that, he would have been accurate, for Webb appeared in his last film, *Satan Never Sleeps*, in 1962 and thereafter retired. But he never did direct a movie and died in 1966. Perhaps he lingered on after his demise because, frustrated at not fulfilling Zanuck's prediction, he found it difficult to settle on the other side.

Other famous ghosts include John Lennon who, in 1981, was murdered by Mark Chapman in the Dakota Building in New York. Musician Joey Harrow and writer Amanda Moores were together when they saw Lennon's ghost standing in the Dakota entrance in 1983. 'He was surrounded by an eerie light,' said Harrow. Amanda Moores recalled, 'I wanted to go up and talk to him, but something in the way he looked at me said *No.*'

Lennon was also seen by Shawn Robbins, a psychic, and, reportedly, by Yoko Ono who saw him sitting at his white piano. He told her, 'Don't be afraid. I am still with you.'

Apparently the most haunted country in the world is Great Britain, or at least, according to the 1971 *Gazetteer of British Ghosts*, 'there are more ghosts seen, reported and accepted in the British Isles than anywhere else on earth'. And it just so happens that some of Britain's most celebrated ghosts reside in historic theatres.

A 'Man in Grey' haunts London's Drury Lane Theatre. It's said that he only manifests himself when the theatre is about to put on a long-running success, which makes him a welcome ghost. He was seen during rehearsals for *Oklahoma!*, *Carousel*, *South Pacific* and *The King and I*. He appears between the hours of 9 am and 6 pm and has been seen by actors and audiences during matinées.

The ghost is said to have been a man of noble birth who lived during the 1770s. He was well known at the theatre, which he frequented as he was in love with an actress who, it seems, had a jealous suitor who stabbed the nobleman to death. The murderer bricked the body into a short and little-used service passage to the left of the stage and there the Man in Grey stayed until his remains were discovered in 1848 when rebuilding work revealed the hidden passage. In his ribs was a Cromwellian-pattern dagger.

Theatre historian W J Macqueen Pope reckoned that the ghost was once seen by 70 members of a cast in rehearsal. He appeared occasionally during the Second World War when Entertainments National Services Association (ENSA) operated from the theatre. But nobody seems able to get closer to him than about 40 feet.

He is described as having powdered hair, and wears a tricorn hat, riding boots, a dress jacket with ruffed sleeves, a long riding cloak and a sword. He enters the auditorium through a wall, passes through some doors leading to the stairs of the upper circle, ascends them and walks around to the other side, comes down another staircase and leaves the auditorium through another part of the wall.

Other ghosts inhabit the Drury Lane Theatre. *Oklahoma!*, in 1947, appears to have attracted its fair share of them when it played there, including King Charles II. He had been a keen theatre-goer in his lifetime and continued into his death.

One of the cast of *Oklahoma!*, American actress Betty Joe Jones, had an important comic part but found that she was not getting the laughs she'd hoped for. Suddenly, while she was in mid-scene, she felt someone gently guiding her around the stage and improving her performance. The invisible presence finally gave her a congratulatory pat on the back.

The same thing happened to Doreen Duke during her audition for *The King and I* in 1954. She felt someone gently patting her on the back, easing her nervousness. After passing the audition, the hands continued to guide her through the tensions of the opening night. This helpful ghost is not the celebrated Man in Grey but is thought by Macqueen Pope to be Joe Grimaldi, the comic and singer who was well loved for his willingness to aid young performers. The Man in Grey makes no sound and keeps himself to himself.

Another ghost at the Drury Lane Theatre is actor Charles Macklin whose short temper led to a brawl with another actor, Thomas Hallam. Macklin killed Hallam but was never jailed for the crime. As he grew older he became thin and ugly, living to the incredible age of 107. Since his death his grotesque figure has been seen in the backstage corridors and it is said that he is doomed to haunt the scene of his unpunished crime.

The Adelphi Theatre in London's Strand is home to the ghost of actor William Terriss who, in December 1897, was stabbed to death as he left the stage door. It is said that his footsteps can be heard and that lights are turned on and off by themselves. The stage lifts move on their own and, in 1928, the couch in what had been his dressing room moved while a startled actress was sitting on it. She had not heard about the ghost and, when her dresser arrived and she told him what had happened, he explained about William Terriss and informed her that she was in his dressing room.

In 1955 Jack Hayden, a ticket collector at Covent Garden Tube station, saw a man in a grey suit and white gloves looking rather lost, so he asked if he could help. The man suddenly vanished. Just four days later a young porter at the station, Victor Locker, felt someone pressing down on his head and looking up saw a man in a grey suit and white gloves. When they were shown photos of Victor Terriss, they recognized him as the ghostly apparition that had appeared to them, and both men instantly asked to be transferred.

Many other members of the Covent Garden Tube station staff have reported feeling a strange presence there, and in 1972 three men – the stationmaster, a signalman and an engineer – all saw William Terriss.

Covent Garden is also the haunt of a ghostly nun who lived at a time when the area was actually Convent Garden. Legend has it that anyone who sees her will have a lucky life. A porter was one day fixing a fuse when the ghostly shape of the nun's face and hands appeared. The legend appears to have worked for that porter. He was Bob Hoskins who quit his job, became an actor and went to Hollywood to become an international star in *Who Framed Roger Rabbit?*.

Perhaps the most famous of Britain's theatre ghosts is the Grey Lady of the Theatre Royal, Bath. Among the many who have seen her was Dame Anna Neagle who told me:

> The Grey Lady was thought to have been an actress during the 1880s who became romantically involved with an admirer who used to watch her every night from one of the boxes. When her husband, also an actor, discovered the affair, he challenged the lover to a duel – a sword fight – and he killed him, straight through the heart. That night, the actress made her last appearance on stage and wore a long grey dress and a headdress of grey feathers. Then she went

to the Garrick's Head Hotel next to the theatre and hanged herself in one of the rooms. She was found the next morning, wearing the grey dress.

Since then her ghost has been seen in the theatre, sometimes sitting in the box from which her lover used to watch her. I saw her, in that box, on the opening night of *The Dame of Sark* [on 23 August 1975]. The curtain went up, I walked on, and I saw her in the box. I had been told I might see her, so it wasn't a surprise, but it still sent the shivers down my back.

The Grey Lady is also said to haunt the Garrick's Head where she died and which was once connected to the theatre by a secret passage. Theatre staff and hotel staff have claimed to have noticed a strong smell of jasmine which they say the Grey Lady leaves wafting behind her. At least three landlords of the Garrick's Head – Peter Welch, Bill Loud and Peter Smith – have claimed to have smelt the jasmine in the cellars. They have also reported phantom knockings on doors, candles flying across the bar, and objects such as money and cuff-links disappearing, only to be discovered in unoccupied rooms.

The Grey Lady has also been seen in Popjoy's Restaurant on the other side of the Theatre Royal. But it is in the theatre itself where the Grey Lady has become such a legend. In June, 1963, a clock, with its mechanism removed, was used on stage as a prop. When its hands reached 12.30 it chimed three times.

During a run of *Blithe Spirit*, a mock seance was carried out to invite the Grey Lady to appear. It was all a publicity stunt, attended by two journalists and the cast, which included Judy Carne, *Laugh-In*'s 'Sock it to me' girl. But the medium who had been hired began to deliver messages.

Judy Carne recalled:

We were all absolutely spellbound, including two cynical newspaper reporters. The voice of a woman told us she had been an actress who had starred at the theatre. She had been married, but had fallen in love with someone else. Her husband and lover fought a duel, and her lover was killed. Heartbroken, she hanged herself in the dressing room. [NB in other accounts, as has been stated, the Grey lady killed herself in the hotel next door.] As I listened, I became very emotional and felt real pain. I tried to talk to her, and asked if she was still unhappy, but the table we were sitting round rattled, and I heard weeping. I often went back to the theatre to try to contact her again, but she never reappeared.

According to Vivienne Rae-Ellis's book *True Ghost Stories of Our Time*, a well-known clairvoyant and ghostbuster spent some time in the theatre, sitting in the box, waiting for the ghostly lady to appear. He reported sensing a 'strong, stubborn and unco-operative presence', but never actually saw her. But many others have, including ballerina Anna Pavlova.

There is another Grey Lady who is resident at the Theatre Royal in York; that city has the reputation for being the most haunted city in Britain. In fact, the *Guinness Book of Records* has described York as 'the most haunted city in Europe'. It was at the Theatre Royal that British actress Julie Dawn Cole, who starred in the BBC TV series *Angels*, saw the Grey Lady while rehearsing on stage one Christmas.

She said, 'I saw her wearing a cloak and a hood. Her outline was iridescent, like gossamer, but I was left with a warm, happy feeling. I consider myself lucky to have seen her.'

In trying to bring a bit of scientific know-how to this book and discover something of the nature of theatre ghosts, I put to you a theory by Dr Percy Seymour of Plymouth University, which suggests that all matter in the universe leaves a 'world-line', or an indelible trace of energy, like a wake of a ship. 'We all leave our footprints on the sands of time,' says Dr Seymour. 'A person of firm and strong habits who has lived at the same place for a very long time would leave a strong "imprint" on the world-lines passing through that place ... and it may be possible for anyone to tune into that image.'

A similar theory favoured by ghost hunters suggests that we

sometimes glimpse visions between two periods of actual time, called 'time-slips'. Apparently these time-slips are more common in Britain than anywhere else in the world, although why this is no one knows. There is also the notion of 'recordings' being replayed according to a series of natural circumstances which may be 'a combination of atmospheric, geological and mental components,' says Peter Underwood.

The Tivoli Theatre in Hull was where actor Arthur Lucan died in his dressing room in 1954. He had been a star of British films and radio and was particularly famous for playing Old Mother Riley in 14 films between 1937 and 1952. One of the series was *Old Mother Riley's Ghosts*, a prophetic title as it happened. He had apparently been in some trouble with the Inland Revenue and had been due, a week after his death, to meet local tax inspectors.

The theatre was later demolished and a tax office erected on its site. Apparently the ghost of Old Mother Riley returned to torment the tax men. One Inland Revenue spokesman said, 'We do not like to say too much about what Old Mother Riley is up to in Hull, but people do stay away from a storeroom on the second floor. There is a strange atmosphere and it is said that the ghost of Mother Riley has been seen.'

Dame Thora Hird, one of the great character and comedy actresses of British films, TV and the stage, had a decidedly uncomfortable ghostly encounter during the run of a Victorian-set play she was in. She had discovered an authentic-looking Victorian jacket in a trunk of theatre jumble and, deciding it was perfect for her role, she tried it for size. It fitted perfectly, so she wore it in the play. Each night it grew tighter. She was sure she was not putting on any weight, but finally the jacket had to be let out by the wardrobe mistress. Said Dame Thora:

One day, my understudy had to wear the jacket. That night, at home after the show, she saw the ghost of a young Victorian woman wearing the same jacket. Later, the wife of the director of the play tried the jacket on, and felt nothing.

But when she took it off, there were red weals on her throat as if someone had tried to strangle her. We decided to get rid of the jacket and a few days later we did. Three mediums held a seance on the stage of the theatre. One had a vision of a girl struggling violently with a man who was tearing at her clothes.

Perhaps it is only fitting that the great star of horror movies, Boris Karloff, is still with us, even though he died in 1969. Towards the end of his life he lived in a cottage called Roundabout in the picturesque village of Bramshot in Hampshire. The village is said to be one of the most haunted in England. A woman called Elizabeth Butler, who drowned herself in 1745, is sometimes seen walking beside the slow-moving stream and the ghost of a little girl in a poke bonnet has been seen leaving the church and disappearing through the churchyard wall.

The old manor house is haunted by an Elizabethan priest, a Quaker, and a White Lady, who is thought to be Lady Hole, one of the house's former owners. Among the many other ghosts in the village are a mounted Cavalier who rides through hedges, a highwayman who rides the lane, and a group of Tudor folk who haunt another leafy lane.

But the most famous of all the village's ghosts is Boris Karloff. Although considered a Hollywood actor, he was actually born in the London suburb of Dulwich in 1887 as William Henry Pratt. He trained initially to become a civil servant in the British foreign service but emigrated to Canada in 1909, where he worked as a farm hand before joining a touring stage company. During a brief stay in Los Angeles in 1916 he landed a film role in *The Dumb Girl of Portici* and when he found himself out of work as a touring actor three years later, he returned to Hollywood. But unable to make enough to live on, he took to driving trucks until he began getting regular parts as villains in films of the 1920s.

After appearing in no fewer than 40 silent films, he finally found fame and fortune as the monster in *Frankenstein* in 1931.

Thus began a staggering career, mainly in horror films, few of which were actually all that good. The film that is generally considered to be one of his best was Peter Bogdanovich's *Targets* (1968) in which he played an ageing star of horror films. It was his last film. The following year he died.

During his last years he lived in his beloved cottage and it is there that he is said to be seen occasionally, looking every inch the gentleman that he was for, despite his screen persona, he was a gentle-mannered man who performed many unpublicized acts of charity for needy children. In death, Boris Karloff is a far less frightening vision than he ever was on the screen when he had bolts in his neck and a scar across his forehead.

Not everyone who believes in the supernatural has actually experienced it first hand, yet remain fascinated and ready to be convinced. That was the attitude of British actress Linda Hayden, who shot to fame in 1969 as the sexy teenage temptress in *Baby Love*. She talked to me about the subject of the paranormal back in 1980 when she shared a flat with her boyfriend, Robin Askwith, star of *Confessions of a Window Cleaner* and other sex comedies of the 1970s.

During a pilgrimage back to Southport where Robin was born, he made a point of showing her the site of the Royal Hotel. Said Linda, 'Robin told me it stood empty for a long time and although it had no electrics or workable machinery, the lift was seen to go up and down.'

It was fascinating to Linda, who had an open mind about these things, while Robin thought it was all a 'load of rubbish'. Linda had no personal experience of ghosts, which I think disappointed her somewhat, but she told me the following chilling story:

A friend of ours was taken by her husband to a country hotel to celebrate their anniversary. She wanted to stay in a particular room because it had a four-poster bed. At about one o'clock in the morning she woke up when she felt someone pushing her down into the bed. She lay there petrified. She woke her husband and told him what had happened and she said that she couldn't spend the night in that room.

He had to take her to the car and drive down the motorway to a transport café to give her some coffee because no one was up in the hotel. At about three o'clock they drove back and sat in the car until it was light before returning to their room.

The next day, before they left, the landlady asked if anything strange happened in the night. He said, 'Like what?' She said, 'The last person who stayed in that room was a vicar who woke up to find someone he couldn't see pushing him into the bed.' She also said that the fingerprints of a child were found on the mirror of that room, even though no child had stayed there for weeks.

They had traced back in the records and discovered that many years ago, a hundred years or so, a little girl died and it was known that this little girl used to try to push her way into her parents' bed.

Those who have seen a ghost and want to know more can join the Ghost Club of Great Britain, as did Peter Sellers, who was obsessed with ghosts and spirits and notions of reincarnation. Peter Underwood recalled how Sellers told him of a series of strange happenings and sounds that occurred while he was filming in Guernsey's famed and reputedly haunted underground bunker. The Nazis had built the bunker during their occupation of the Channel Islands during the Second World War as a military hospital and ammunition store.

Underwood told Sellers that an unknown number of slave labourers had died and were left to rot in the bunker, while a further 54 were buried nearby. The locals never went there and visitors often found the place disturbing, some being reduced to tears. Sellers told Peter Underwood that he had never been so frightened anywhere in his life.

Before Sellers was a famous film star, he was one of the Goons on BBC Radio, with Harry Secombe, Spike Milligan and the 'forgotten Goon', Michael Bentine. While Sellers became obsessed with spiritualism, Bentine was virtually born into it, being the son of a Peruvian psychic called Adam Bentine who was well known among British entertainers. During the Second World War, Michael Bentine served as an Intelligence officer with the RAF. One evening he was returning to his base at Wickenby after a taking a two-day leave of absence, when he saw his good friend, a flight-lieutenant known to everyone as 'Pop'. Pop had just finished his tour of 30 operations and was due to stand down. Bentine, heading for his hut, was on an interception course with Pop who was on his way to his own Nissen hut. It was late, almost midnight.

Bentine waved and said, 'Hi, Pop!' Pop acknowledged him and continued on past towards his hut. The only thing that made Bentine feel that something was odd was a sudden chill he felt. He continued towards the hut and got into bed.

The next morning he was awakened by his batman with a cup of tea and the words, 'Bloody shame about Pop. Finished his tour an' all. Bloody bad luck, sir.'

Bentine asked him what he meant. The batman explained that Pop had volunteered to fly with a new crew and that the plane had crashed into the woods at night. It happened on the day Bentine left for his leave.

'I saw him last night,' said Bentine.

'You must have been mistaken about seeing him last night, sir,' the batman insisted.

But Bentine was always sure he did see Pop.

It is not often that film sets are said to be haunted. Recently, an American couple rented the video of *Three Men and a Baby* and were were shocked when they saw the ghost of their son in a scene in the film. At least, they were convinced it was their son's ghost. They had lived in the apartment used in the film and the boy had died some years before Ted Danson, Tom Sellick and Steve Guttenberg were filmed there, playing three bachelors bringing up a baby.

The couple were sure they saw their boy standing by a window, partly hidden by the net curtains. And the figure is definitely visible in one shot of the film as the camera pans past the window. Somebody, or something, is definitely standing there, and it does look like a boy.

A stir was caused when the matter was taken up on America's *60 Minutes* show in which the couple insisted that the figure is the ghost of their son.

A spokesperson for Disney, the film's distributor, said, 'There is no ghost. It's a standee. The film makers were really very amused when they heard references to a ghost. They just said, "Gee no, it's just a prop".'

The standee, a large-sized cardboard cut-out, is said to be of Ted Danson. When asked what it was doing there, the spokesperson replied,

> Well, you see, in the sequel Danson plays an actor and he's forever being depicted as a character other than himself. In one of the opening montages of the sequel Danson sits in the back of a prop truck next to a standee of himself in character and it's supposed to be funny because he's gesturing in the same way as the standee. And maybe, in [director] Leonard Nimoy's mind the prop in part was a reference to the sequel; perhaps that's where he got the idea.

Not surprisingly, this explanation did little to persuade the couple since there was no clear explanation as to how a standee from the sequel turns up in the first film. However, this is one ghost story that can be laid to rest, thanks to *Empire* magazine who were able to establish that the figure was indeed a cardboard cut-out of Ted Danson. They noted, however, 'a satisfactory reason for its being there in the first place has yet to be suggested.'

The former Bushey film studios in Hertfordshire was haunted. It was opened in the early days of cinema when the British film industry *was* an industry (although it reverted to being a TV studio in the early 1960s). Shortly after it was opened, two starlets reported for work and were scared witless when they saw a luminous, blue aristocratic lady walk across a darkened sound stage. The Blue Lady turned out to be Lulu, the wife of Baron von Herkomer whose country mansion had stood on the site of the new studio.

Actual locations for films may sometimes turn out to be haunted, as in the case of *Some Like It Hot*, the classic Billy Wilder comedy of 1958. Much of the film was shot on location at the Hotel del Coronado, in San Diego, California. Room 502 has the reputation for being haunted and is usually left empty as no one wants to spend the night there. When Tony Curtis, Jack Lemmon and Marilyn Monroe were filming there, they and all concerned with the film avoided that room. The last thing Billy Wilder wanted was a ghost messing up his expensive production.

Real ghosts were to be found on the set of the British TV series *Dick Turpin*, which told the adventures of the legendary highwayman. I had not been forewarned that I might come across a few spooks when I went to cover the filming of the series for *Photoplay*.

I arrived at Ockwell Manor in Maidenhead, where *Dick Turpin* was being filmed, in the summer of 1978. I had gone there particularly to interview the star of the series, Richard O'Sullivan, best remembered by British audiences from the 1970s situation comedies *Man About the House* and *Robin's Nest*. American audiences would know him better as Elizabeth Taylor's brother in *Cleopatra*.

Ockwell Manor had been built in the fourteenth century. By 1978, it had been completely restored, complete with oak beams, leaning walls, crooked doorways, outhouses, a beautiful garden and stables. For *Dick Turpin* the whole place had been transformed into a small studio for the duration of filming.

I made my way to the producer's office where I found, not the producer, but his secretary. A nice girl, full of good advice such as, 'See that door opposite? You don't want to go in there.' She was pointing to a large wooden door opposite her office. I asked her why I wouldn't want to go in that room. 'Because Henry VI used to hang people in that room,' she answered.

'Oh, I'd like to see that,' I said enthusiastically, and headed towards it.

'Don't say I didn't warn you. People steer clear of that room.'

I stopped in my tracks and asked, 'Why do they?'

'Because it's haunted.'

I had never believed in ghosts. And I did not intend to start believing now. But I decided not to tempt fate and, heeding her advice – just in case – I went in search of Richard O'Sullivan. The producer's secretary was my guide through the grounds. We passed a gate which appeared to lead to the gardens. I pointed to it and said, 'Can we go in there?'

Again came the advice, 'You don't want to go in there.' I was beginning to wonder if there was anywhere in this place I would want to go. She went on to explain that she had gone walking in the gardens in the previous week and had suddenly felt an icy chill. Two days later she mentioned this incident to an inhabitant of the manor who informed her that someone had been decapitated in the garden and the head had been buried somewhere in the grounds. Many people had claimed to see the head floating about the garden. She had not seen it, but she had felt a chilling presence.

So again I heeded the warning and eventually found Richard O'Sullivan mounted on his trusty steed, Black Bess – or at least the horse that was playing the part of Black Bess. But as the cameras 'turned', the horse refused to take the exact given direction. It took several attempts before the director decided he had got all the takes he needed.

Richard O'Sullivan slipped down from his horse and dropped into a webbed chair. I asked him various questions about the series, his acting, his horse-riding prowess and sword-fighting abilities. Then we got down to the serious subject of the manor's numerous ghosts. He told me,

I've heard quite a few tales about Ockwell. I can tell you, we don't like to stay in this place too long. We were talking to someone the other day who said that Turpin used to charge around Maidenhead Thicket, and that his ghost sometimes appears. People say that they hear hoofs thundering around the Thicket late at night. Now, whether Turpin actually went to Ockwell Manor, I don't know, but the place has a history all of its own.

A number of people on the location had tales to tell. One of the crew said he had heard the phantom hoofbeats of Black Bess. I told him he was pulling my leg. He was adamant he wasn't. I was beginning to feel relieved that I had not been sent to cover a night shoot. I was then told that in the nearby village of Apsley Guise, just a mile south of the M1, stands a house called Woodfield. It is supposedly haunted by Dick Turpin and Black Bess, and a young woman and her lover.

The story told to me was that the girl's father was a strict Puritan who had forbidden her to dally with the local lads. But the lusty girl broke the rules and entertained numerous willing lads while her father was away on business. Unfortunately, he came home unexpectedly and found her in the arms of a young man who had become her lover.

In his righteous indignation, the father barred the room with them inside by pushing heavy furniture against the door. And there he left them to their fate.

It just so happened that Dick Turpin later turned up at Woodfield, broke in and discovered the bodies. Since he was not exactly a man of high morals, he blackmailed the master of the house into giving him sanctuary from time to time – or Turpin threatened to reveal the father's terrible secret. Turpin even helped the father to bury the bodies under the floor of the cellar.

The ghosts of the lovers began to haunt the house and later the ghost of Dick Turpin joined them. To this day he rides around the grounds of Woodfield on Black Bess, occasionally putting in an appearance up at Ockwell Manor.

My day was over and I went away to write my story for *Photoplay*. But some weeks later, when a feature-length special of *Dick Turpin* was being filmed, I went back. Former glamour screen queen Diana Dors was there that day, making a cameo appearance, and I found that she, as someone who had a ghost of her own at home, was sensitive to the ghostly vibes.

In the end I decided I really did want to see all the places the producer's secretary was sure I did not want to see. I had always been a rational person, not given to believing in ghosts, and I decided I would have a wander in the beautiful rose gardens. The sun was warm and the flowers smelt sweet. It was a most beautiful setting. Then it grew cold. Not just cool, but an icy chill that really did send my neck hairs to attention. But I saw no head. Not that I gave myself much time to look for it. I got out of there pretty quickly and the cold chill left me.

Feeling relatively brave now, it seemed only right that I should go to have a look in the room opposite the producer's office where Henry VI had stretched a neck or two. The room was heavily beamed and really very attractive, and in that sense it seemed no different to most of the other rooms in the manor. Except this one was extremely cold. Entering it was a bit like walking into a fridge. I could not tell you much more about the room because I did not stay a second longer.

That day at Ockwell Manor remains my only near encounter with what may or may not have been a ghost or two. I do not claim that there were any ghostly apparitions that day and it may well be there are natural explanations for the icy chill that I felt in the garden and the cold air of that room. But I didn't go back to Ockwell.

3

The Stars Who Died and Lived to Tell

Near death experience (NDE) is a phenomenon which, so far, has plenty of anecdotal evidence but nothing concrete to prove it is real. But for those who have experienced it, it is a journey into death – and life. NDE occurs when people are brought to the very brink of death, either by illness or an accident, and are so far gone they are not expected to survive. Usually the heart stops and breathing ceases. There is just a short space of time before the brain dies, after which further attempts at resuscitation are useless. Those who are brought back and revived before the final crucial moment often have a remarkable story to tell.

One of these people is Elizabeth Taylor. The phenomenon happened to her when she was in the process of portraying the legendary Queen of Egypt, Cleopatra.

Cleopatra was to be the biggest motion picture of all time. There had already been a number of a false starts to get Walter Wanger's epic production for 20th Century-Fox under way since 1958. It finally began in September 1960, under the direction of Rouben Mamoulian at Pinewood Studios. Elizabeth Taylor starred as Cleopatra, Peter Finch was Julius Caesar and Stephen Boyd was Mark Antony. But after almost two months of filming, production was halted as Taylor was stricken by a series of viruses.

This gave Mamoulian the opportunity to try to improve the rather dire script but, before he could acquire a more satisfactory version, 20th Century-Fox ordered filming to resume on 3

January 1961. After a series of behind-the-scenes disagreements, Mamoulian resigned on 18 January and was replaced by Joseph L Mankiewicz, who arrived at Pinewood on 1 February, viewed the exposed footage and said he would have to re-shoot everything. Fox gave him until 4 April to get shooting under way again. Then, on 1 March, Elizabeth Taylor came down with another virus and was ordered to bed in her suite at the Dorchester Hotel in London. Her condition deteriorated and by the night of 3 March she had developed severe respiratory difficulties. Doctors were immediately summoned to her suite and in the morning she was rushed to the London Clinic where she was diagnosed as having pneumonia complicated by a staphylococcal infection.

She underwent an emergency tracheotomy, but doctors and surgeons held out little hope for her survival. They informed her husband, Eddie Fisher, that she was dying. Wanger and Mankiewicz hurried to the Clinic where they kept vigil with a disconsolate Eddie Fisher.

For two days Liz slipped in and out of a coma, growing increasingly weak in the intensive care unit. Eddie told reporters outside the Clinic, 'I'm going to lose my girl.'

Sackfuls of letters arrived from thousands of well-wishers. One, from America, read, 'Six thousand of us are praying for you here at the Boeing plant.' A submarine crew in the Indian Ocean wired, 'Don't give up, Liz.'

But it seemed hopeless as she weakened to the point that her heart stopped. Doctors fought to get it beating again. They succeeded and, gradually, Liz began to recover. By 12 March she was sitting up in bed receiving visitors. Eddie Fisher finally allowed himself to believe that he would not, after all, lose his girl.

Taylor talked publicly for the first time of the experience in July 1961 at a fund-raising dinner for Cedars of Lebanon-Mount Sinai Hospital (now called more simply Cedars of Lebanon). She told the thousand-strong audience who had each paid $2,500 to hear her speak:

Dying is many things, but most of all, it is wanting to live.
Throughout many critical hours in the operating theatre, it
was as if every nerve, every muscle were being strained to
the last ounce of my strength. Gradually and inevitably, that
last ounce was drawn, and there was no more breath. I
remember I had focused desperately on the hospital light
hanging directly above me. It had become something I
needed almost fanatically to continue to see – the vision of
life itself. Slowly it faded and dimmed, like a well-done
theatrical effect, to blackness.

I died. Shall I tell you what it was like? Being down a
long, dark tunnel, and there was a small light at the end. I
had to keep looking at that light. And I heard the voices,
urging me to come back, come back.

The experience I had was painful, but beautiful too. It was
like childbirth – painful but so beautiful.

Many years later, when I had the chance to meet her at a press
call, she said, 'I remember feeling an enormous peace, like I was
floating easily on warm and calm water. I was no longer a part of
my body, or it was no longer a part of me, and I was hovering
over the bed. I learned later that I had died.'

As a postscript to this tale, filming on *Cleopatra* was brought to
a complete halt while Liz recovered, during which time it was
decided to move the whole production to Rome where the
climate was better suited to her. Filming resumed in October
1961, and finished on 5 March 1963. Peter Finch and Stephen
Boyd, who were unable to wait indefinitely for the new start date
had to drop out and were replaced by, respectively, Rex Harrison
and Richard Burton. And with the arrival of Burton, as
Hollywood history knows, Eddie Fisher did, in the end, lose his
girl.

The big question that preoccupies many of us – apart from
why did it take so long to film *Cleopatra*? – is, is there life after
death? Elizabeth Taylor had joined an exclusive club of people
who are convinced there is. Membership of this club involves
undergoing NDE. Liz Taylor's story of what happened to her

when she passed away, albeit briefly – of looking down a dark tunnel, seeing a light, being out of the body and hovering over the bed – is very typical of most who undergo NDE. These survivors often talk of feeling at peace, of being relieved and not always wanting to go back. This, they say, is what death is like.

Whether it is or not is an ongoing question that continues to be argued. For those who experience it, there seems no question at all. Erik Estrada, the star of the 1970s TV series *CHIPS*, was the victim of a motorcycle crash. He was severely injured and for a few moments his heart stopped. He was lucky to be revived, although he may feel that he would not have been particularly unfortunate to have given in to death. He recalled, 'There was a long corridor, lots of bright lights, beautiful music and a feeling of great peace. But I felt something seemed to be blocking my progress. A voice told me, "You've got to go back – you've a lot still to do".'

Peter Sellers had a similar experience when he suffered a major heart attack on a sound stage at the Goldwyn Studios in Hollywood in 1964. Fifteen years later, when he found himself back on that sound stage to make *Being There*, he told his co-star Shirley Maclaine, 'This is the sound stage where I died. Rex Kennamer saved my life, and I saw him do it.'

He told her that when he died, he felt himself leave his body. He floated up and watched his body being taken away to hospital. He went with it, he said, because he was curious. He wanted to know what was wrong with him. But he did not feel frightened; he felt just fine as he was.

Rex Kennamer was the doctor who felt for Sellers's pulse and discovered it had stopped. All the while, Sellers was watching as Kennamer and the other doctors fought to save him. He said, 'They did everything but jump up and down on me to get my heart beating again.'

He heard Dr Kennamer say that there was no time to prepare him for heart surgery and quickly opened Sellers's chest to massage the heart by hand. Sellers remembered, 'I was so curious watching him. He just refused to accept that I was dead.'

Then, said Sellers, he saw 'an incredibly beautiful bright

loving white light' above him, and he felt he wanted to go to that light more than anything else. 'I knew there was love, real love, on the other side of the light.' He saw a hand reaching out towards him from the light, and he tried to move towards it. But he could not make reach it, and he heard Dr Kennamer say, 'It's beating again. I'm getting a heartbeat.'

He heard another voice coming from the direction of the hand, saying, 'It's not time. Go back and finish. It's not time.'

The hand disappeared and Sellers, disappointed, felt himself return to his body. After that, he knew nothing until he regained consciousness.

Sellers's *Goon* companion, Michael Bentine, also underwent a near death experience. He described the experience as being in 'the endless, boundless, infinite presence of God.' It happened during the Second World War while Bentine was serving in the RAF. He had to be given one of a series of inoculations that induced a severe fever. Before long he grew delirious and experienced severe pain. He was put into hospital and his wife and parents were summoned; the doctor did not expect Michael to survive.

In his book, *The Door Marked Summer*, Bentine recalls how, at the point of almost unbearable pain, he felt himself released from his body. He gave up the struggle to survive readily as he was overcome with 'an awe-filled acceptance at the naturalness of the process'. He said that he found himself 'standing in the presence of eternity', and felt aware that 'this was reality and all else an illusion'. He wrote that it was on a scale so immense that it passed all understanding. He recalled standing, his arms outstretched, in the presence of God.

Then he felt himself drawn back and returned to his body. He opened his eyes and saw people sitting around his bed. A nursing sister told him, 'You've been a long way.'

He found he could not speak immediately and listened as two military chaplains argued over who would administer to him. One said, 'His father's Peruvian or something. He must be Catholic.' The other argued, 'Church of England. It says so on his documents. He's mine.'

Both chaplains leaned over the bed, looking benignly at the semi-conscious Bentine; they could see he wanted to speak. The Catholic priest crossed himself and asked, 'Yes, my son?' The other smiled and asked, 'What is it, lad?'

With a great effort, Bentine found his voice and croaked, 'Piss off! I'm alive!'

Bentine later observed of his NDE, 'My soul had experienced eternity'. He has had a number of other brushes with death throughout his life, but through his NDE experience and his insight into the paranormal, he has remained unafraid of death.

Elizabeth Taylor, Erik Estrada, Peter Sellers and Michael Bentine are just a small handful of people, and perhaps the most famous, who are convinced they died and came back again. Since 1975 thousands of similar stories have been systematically collected, although there are recorded incidents of NDE in ancient Tibetan and Egyptian books. Even Plato, the Greek philosopher, described the phenomenon. But there are those today who do not believe that the visions these people see are real events, and have offered possible explanations. Foremost perhaps among sceptics is Dr Susan Blackmore from the Department of Psychology at the University of Western England.

In a nutshell, she maintains that these experiences – leaving the body, looking down on themselves, being pulled into a tunnel, seeing a light – are just hallucinations, induced by endorphins which are the body's own opium-type chemicals. As cells in the optic neurone network exhaust their oxygen, they fire randomly and increase in speed. There are more cells in the centre of vision than on the periphery, and the result is what appears to be a bright light at the centre of darkness, hence the tunnel and the light at the end. The feeling of complete reality, she says, is due to the brain seizing on this retinal firing as the only stable element in a rapidly deteriorating process, and this makes the experience seem real to the dying person.

Not all sceptics agree with her theory and there are many other possible explanations, all of which to the layman like myself seem equally feasible. Dr Elisabeth Kubler-Ross, a pioneer in terminal medical care, believes that those pronounced clinically dead – when their heart stops – know what is going on around them because their brains are still alive. Or, as she puts it, 'The dying patient continues to have a conscious awareness of his environment after being pronounced clinically dead.'

According to neuropsychiatrist Dr Peter Fenwick, there are, almost without exception, at least two responses common to those who experience NDE: 'Most people lose their fear of death. A lot of people feel that they have a mission that they have to go through. There is something for them to do in this life.' This is something that apparently bothered Peter Sellers, and became an obsession. He felt he had been brought back for some purpose but he could never quite grasp what that was. It was just one of his obsessions that drove his life and career – and drove many around him – up the wall. He also believed in reincarnation, which contributed to his Quixotic quest to discover what he was supposed to do. It was all part of what some have described as his genius and others as his madness.

4

Messages from the Other Side

In December 1980, a shot rang out in the Dakota Building in New York, ending the life of John Lennon. Ever since then Lennon has been conspicuous by his presence twixt this world and the next.

As one of the Beatles, Lennon appeared in a handful of films: *A Hard Day's Night*, *Help!* and *Magical Mystery Tour* in the 1960s. Director Richard Lester, who made the first two films, told me that Lennon always thought that acting was silly despite being a natural actor. He therefore did not pursue an acting career although he did give it a single shot in Lester's 1967 black comedy *How I Won the War*. The surviving Beatles have all had forays into films. Paul McCartney did not quite make it big at the box office with *Give My Regards To Broad Street* and Ringo Starr has had variable success as an actor in the Italian western *Blindman*, the musical *That'll Be the Day* and the bizarre *The Magic Christian*. George Harrison had the foresight to ignore acting and to set up Handmade Films, which produced a number of highly successful films including Monty Python's *Life of Brian*.

But back to Lennon's progress since his death. As well as his aforementioned ghostly appearances (see pages 18–19), he has been in touch with various mediums and Spiritualists on both sides of the Atlantic. In John Lennon, we have what appears to be a case of a ghost crossing over from one stage of death to another. In contradiction to those who consider ghosts to be 'recordings' from the past, or persons caught in 'time-slips',

41

there are those who claim that a ghost is someone who will not 'let go' after their death. These ghosts seem left in some kind of limbo to haunt the place of their demise, which I suppose is the opinion most people have of ghosts. According to Bill Harry in *Idols* magazine, some Spiritualists have said that Lennon's spirit lingered on Earth for a short time before his 'spirit guides' helped him to adjust to the 'other world'. From the time he entered the spirit world, he began sending messages to this world through various mediums.

The first contact with Lennon came through Linda Deer Domnitz in California just four days after his death. Over a period of 26 months Linda Deer Domnitz spoke to Lennon, taping her conversations with him and making them available in book and audio tape form as *The John Lennon Conversations*. He told her that he remains close to the earth in order to save it from destruction. His mission in death, as in life, is to further the cause of world peace and harmony.

In 1988 she wrote to Bill Harry to reveal that she was still receiving contact from Lennon and that he was sending messages to the three surviving Beatles. To Paul he said:

> You can create a whole new type of music which has been somewhat alien to you in the past and which you considered my bag. I would like you to consider it now your bag, as I am transferring it to you and hope that you will understand what I am trying to tell you and how much you can be the focus for this type of New Age music which will help bring us all back together again as one family in the world of peace for all mankind.

To Ringo he said:

> I want you to know that I am at peace, Ringo, and I am happy to be where I am. I have no regrets and no animosities toward anyone, so let that go and bear no grudges to anyone you think may have wronged me because I feel no such hatred or animosity. There is no one I love more than you. You have been a constant companion and a

faithful friend, and I appreciate very sincerely all your help, your kindness to Yoko and all of your admiration.

To George:

I hope that you will emulate some of the things which I have taught you, especially in the peace movement, but that you will not be a clone for me any more than I was a clone for anyone else. I want your ideas to be original, and clear, and concise, and to the point, so that everyone hearing your music can understand exactly where you are coming from and where you've been. This is not John Lennon but George Harrison, although there are some similarities. You are you, and I am me, but we can work together as we have in the past.

What the Beatles' response has been to these messages has not been made public. But there is good news for Elvis Presley fans too, for Lennon told Deer Domnitz that he has seen Elvis and talked at great length about their music and about the after life. 'He is with his mother, father and brother,' says Lennon, 'and they're happy as two peas in a pod.' Perhaps Lennon was never very good with sums.

Yet to be discovered are papers which, Lennon told Deer Domnitz, he spent much time writing concerning his thoughts on what death would be like. He says, 'When these papers are discovered it will be noted that I had no hesitancy about embracing death, although I loved life more dearly.'

In Wimbledon, London, a medium called Rosemary Brown began receiving messages from Lennon in her living room in 1984. Specifically, he dictated more than two dozen new songs to her. She claims that he comes in spirit form which she can see, and described him as 'taller than I always imagined him in this life. I seem to see him as he looked at the height of the Beatles' early success – he looks in his late twenties or so, is clean shaven, fresh-faced, doesn't wear glasses.'

She says that he was surprised by a continuing process of learning and evolving on the other side. 'He told me that the after life is very much a continuation of this life. You pick up where you left off. You don't suddenly change or know everything.'

He also told her that he still loves Cynthia, his first wife, and that he wants his son Julian to record the songs he has passed on to Rosemary Brown.

Cynthia Lennon has had her own experience that John is still about, but not through any visitation. In 1986, she found a dead jackdaw wrapped in old newspapers dated 1956 behind the fireplace of her house in Cumbria. She told Annette Witheridge of the *Sunday Mirror*, 'John told Julian that if there was life after death he would prove it by sending a feather as a sign. When Julian saw the jackdaw he was really shaken. It's as if John is trying to get in touch with us.'

John once gave Julian an Indian headdress. Someone managed to get their hands on it and the first Cynthia realized it was missing was when she heard it was on sale. As trustee of Julian's property, she fought and won a court case to retrieve it, and presented it to him just before he gave his first major concert at the Royal Albert Hall. 'The show was a great success,' said Cynthia who, if reports are to believed, saw this as another connection to John's promise to his son to send a feather after his death.

Another medium who claims to have spoken to Lennon is Bill Tenuto of San Diego. He says he learned that John had been reunited with his mother, Julia. 'She's so beautiful,' Lennon told Tenuto. He has also met Jesus. 'He's a spirit. He's a great person. He's a master.'

Tenuto claims that Lennon held a party in the spirit world and among the guests were Clark Gable and Carole Lombard. Lennon said he 'really took to her [Lombard]. We are capable of having sex over here. We do the same thing that you do except without the body. We love sex as much as anybody who's got a body. The sensations are a bit different, with an interplay of energies that takes place when we have sex. We don't concern ourselves with Planned Parenthood since the spirits can't propagate a baby spirit.' Which is just as well since Lennon appears to have been quite promiscuous on the other side. During a break in his sessions with Tenuto, Lennon took up with what he described as 'a female energy-type spirit person and we went off and made it. It was a quickie. It was quite nice. It energized me.'

Promiscuity is apparently not a sin in the spirit world because, says Tenuto, Lennon has joined the White Brotherhood, a group of highly advanced spirits whose work is to communicate the messages of the Masters to the political leaders of the world. Another spirit in league with the White Brotherhood is John Wayne.

Like Deer Domnitz, Tenuto released his conversations with Lennon on tape, but Yoko Ono successfully banned them. Interestingly, Jenny Randles, author of *The Paranormal Year Book*, writes in the 1993 edition that she tried to get Cynthia Lennon to listen to the tapes in an effort to help judge the merits of the evidence. Cynthia, however, turned her down. Randles went on to write that she does 'personally believe the medium [Tenuto] is sincere, whatever the interpretation we place upon his story.'

It is, of course, easy to scoff at all of these claims if you are not inclined to believe in Spiritualism. And even if you do you may have doubts as to whether any or all of these claims are made purely with commercial profit in mind. I try not to close my mind to any possibilities but I do wonder about one or two things. They may have occurred to you too. For instance, if John Lennon was helped from his ghostly form to his spirit form by guides so as to be in communication with Linda Deer Domnitz only four days after his death, how did his ghost come to be seen so often in the ensuing years? Another contradiction between stories is that Rosemary Brown says that she sees John not wearing glasses, whereas in Deer Domnitz's book *The John Lennon Conversations* there are pictures by artist Susan Rowe showing Lennon wearing specs.

Doris Stokes, the celebrated British medium, was also contacted by John Lennon during a session for a girl whom Mrs Stokes simply called 'Annie' in her book *Innocent Voices in My Ear*.

Annie had become involved in a business project and had given up her job, her flat, everything she had to finance the business, but nothing seemed to be happening. So she consulted Doris Stokes who, during the course of the session, heard a voice say, 'My name is John Lennon.'

He went on to say that Annie had been talking to his friend Elton John the previous evening; and Annie said she had. It turned out she used to be in the music business, although she had never met John Lennon. Nevertheless, John advised Annie to ask Yoko Ono for help in her business venture. He also went on to say he had met Brian Epstein, the Beatles' manager who killed himself, and Brian Jones, the Rolling Stones drummer, who was found dead in a swimming pool.

Mrs Stokes asked Lennon about his feelings towards Mark Chapman and Lennon replied that he had no bitterness. 'He wasn't right in the head, was he?' Lennon said with a laugh. He also told Doris that he had shown himself to his son Sean.

Mrs Stokes did not give any indication as to whether Lennon's advice to Annie paid off or not. But I am baffled that Doris Stokes said that Lennon spoke not with a Liverpudlian but an American accent. I was interested to come across a book by British medium James Byrne in which he touched on the subject of contact with legendary stars on the other side. He said, 'I can think of no reason why people I have no connection with, film stars or anyone else, should try and contact me ... I laugh when I read about such and such a medium speaking with Elvis. Why would he want to do that? The answer is, he simply wouldn't, it's just a very good story.'

In defence of Doris Stokes (and here I am playing devil's advocate), she was very friendly with many celebrities, so she may well be considered something of a specialist in star-studded Spiritualism. She also said that while she would have loved to talk to the spirits of many famous people, including Winston Churchill, President Kennedy and Elvis Presley, there was no reason why they would talk to a stranger.

One of Doris Stokes's good friends was Diana Dors, Britain's own blonde bombshell of the 1950s. Born with the unfortunate name of Diana Fluck, she was renamed Diana Dors by Rank who signed her to a ten-year contract in 1947 at the bargain basement price of £10 a week. In 1955 she signed a new contract with Rank, reputedly worth £100,000, who tried to mould her as Britain's answer to Marilyn Monroe. She hated this whole idea but had no choice and was delighted to shed her glamorous image to star as a girl-gone-wrong on Britain's death row in *Yield to the Night* in 1956. She had proved that she was more than just a pretty face and a voluptuous body.

She went to Hollywood where RKO purchased her contract from Rank, but she later sued the studio for more than a million dollars charging that she had 'become an object of disgrace, ill-will and ridicule'. They settled out of court in 1960 for $200,000. That put paid to her Hollywood career, so she returned to Britain and made occasional forays into European productions.

By the late 1960s she had become obese and audiences wondered what had happened to her hour-glass figure. Apparently she had a medical condition which accounted for her weight problem. That paled into insignificance when she was diagnosed with cancer during the early 1980s.

She was married for the third time, to actor Alan Lake, and they lived in a house that was reputedly haunted; the ghost did not bother the Lakes. Doris Stokes claimed that while she was chatting to Diana and Alan Lake at a reception thrown by Robert Maxwell, she had the feeling that something was wrong with Diana. Shortly afterwards Dors was admitted to hospital with a stomach complaint. Released for a short time, she was soon back in again for an emergency operation. Doris Stokes was convinced she would not make it and she was right. Diana Dors died in 1984.

Doris Stokes said that Diana came through to her shortly after her death, saying, 'Tell Alan I'm only a whisper away, and that Minnie met me.'

Mrs Stoke rang Alan Lake and told her the news; Minnie, it turned out, was Lake's mother. But this did not comfort him and, stricken with grief, he shot himself.

When Diana and Alan's fifteen-year-old son, Jason, told Doris that he was going to America, she assured him that his mother was watching over him. At that moment, she heard Diana's voice say, 'You'd better believe it.'

The whole subject of Spiritualism fascinated me when I was a child. My best friend's mother, who became very interested in the subject, used to conduct sessions using a method familiar to many, with an upturned glass and a large circle of letters. The 'spirit of the glass' spelled out its messages. When I asked what I would be when I grew up, it spelled out 'film producer'. So far I have not achieved this ambition.

Peter Finch is another film star who has come through to Doris Stokes. The Australian hellraiser died of a heart attack in 1977 after a life of hard drinking, hard loving and hardly any time to devote to being a husband. Doris Stokes had never met him, but his second former wife, Yolande, and their daughter, Samantha, came to Mrs Stokes to seek contact with him.

His spirit came through and said that their divorce had been a mistake, and he seemed to blame Yolande for wanting the divorce. 'We should have worked things out,' Finch said through Mrs Stokes. 'You would have been my salvation.' Finch explained that he had hit the bottle hard because of his fear of failing. Then Yolande's father came through, as well as other members of the family. It turned into quite a reunion. Finch returned to the subject of the divorce, and he and Yolande engaged in a blazing row. At one point Doris asked Finch to modify his strong language, since she was the one passing on his words. The session ended amicably as Finch expressed his love for his family and regret at the failed marriage.

In writing of this session in *More Voices in My Ear*, Mrs Stokes gave no clue as to what the row was about, except that Finch accused Yolande of nagging, and she replied that she nagged him for his own good. There was no mention of the fact that Yolande had divorced Finch in 1965 because of his admitted adultery.

I have no doubt that many mediums are sincere in what they do. What their source of information is, what these 'spirits' are, may or may not be those who have departed. I recall that when I went on the location for the 1979 series of *Quatermass* which starred John Mills, I got chatting to one of the walk-on actors, who told me he was a medium and had been in touch with Marilyn Monroe. She told him why she had taken her own life. In 1979 I knew little enough about the events surrounding Monroe's death to question him.

The subject of Monroe's suicide came up again some years later during a TV interview with Doris Stokes who said that she had asked Monroe why she killed herself. Monroe replied that she had been depressed and upset, and gave all the usual reported reasons that were published when her death was first announced. By this time I did know more about Monroe's death and the events surrounding it. From all I have been told, read and heard, I have no doubt that Monroe did not take her own life (as I explain in *The Hollywood Murder Casebook* and *The Hollywood Connection*). So I wonder why Monroe would admit to suicide? Yet I try not to be sceptical and, as a lifelong fan of John Wayne, I take some comfort in the prospect that he may be out there working alongside John Lennon, putting the world to rights by delivering spiritual messages to the world's leaders.

Life after death does not, it seems, always prove to be a peaceful and restful experience. Vivien Leigh, who died on 7 July 1967 was, it was reported, deeply unhappy during the first weeks of her time on the other side. It would be easy to make light of this but for the fact that, as the story unfolds, it touches the heart of anyone who has in some way been touched by her life and work.

And just about everyone who has seen *Gone With the Wind* would agree that the spoilt, selfish and often ruthless Scarlett O'Hara, as portrayed by Vivien Leigh, remains the greatest heroine of any film. But the Vivien Leigh film that really struck an emotional chord in me for days after I saw it was *Waterloo Bridge* in which she played a prostitute, in love with Robert Taylor but unable to live up to his family's expectations of respectability. In the end, she throws herself under the wheels of a vehicle on Waterloo Bridge where she had met him.

She won the hearts of cinema-goers as she won the heart of Laurence Olivier, her husband from 1940 to 1960. As a couple, they were loved by the public, although towards the end of their marriage their lives were being torn apart by her deteriorating mental state. She made his life hell but she was half out of her mind much of the time and it is impossible to put her deplorable behaviour down to plain cruelty or bitchiness. Their marriage ended in divorce.

In her final years, when she was married to John 'Jack' Merrivale, her mental state improved, but her physical state did not. She finally succumbed to tuberculosis.

Not long after, in October 1976, Gertrude Hartley, Vivien's mother, and Jack Merrivale received a surprise letter from Consuelo Mangton-Lockton, an astrologer who had cast Vivien's horoscopes as far back as 1938. She announced that she was willing to be used as a channel for any messages which Vivien might wish to send from the other side. Consuelo found a medium on the south coast of England near Bexhill and, during a seance, a number of spirits made their presence known before Vivien came through. She was, according to the medium, 'very indistinct – she is very tired – *very* tired – she is absolutely exhausted – she tries to wake, but cannot – she floats as on a river which bears her up – very, very tired.'

Vivien seemed to be a very sad spirit, not at all happy and relieved to have passed through to the other side. She could remember her death, of feeling a great weight on her chest, then a sharp, piercing pain near her heart – and then she died. She was anxious to make it clear that she did not commit suicide. She was also upset that she was cut off from those she loved. When Consuelo reported this to Jack, he thought it was very like Vivien to dislike being isolated.

Two weeks later another seance was held. Vivien's spirit came through and recalled a terrible party at which Consuelo had arranged a surprise. Vivien had thought the surprise was going to be the arrival of Laurence Olivier who had been away and whom she greatly missed. But instead the surprise was a village band which played just for her. She had cried with disappointment and the band was sent away.

Consuelo later found another medium through whom Vivien continually asked how Olivier was, and begged his forgiveness. She was desperate to let him know she still loved him. Consuelo realized that it was Olivier who was drawing Vivien back to the physical world, preventing her from finding peace in the spirit world. The medium told Gertrude, 'If he should go, she will be waiting. Love is stronger than death – and things get sorted out on that side. Thank God.'

Olivier has gone now. If what Consuelo reported was true, it would be too awful to contemplate the emotional consequences on the living let alone the dead. But beyond that sort of speculation, the vision of Vivien Leigh existing in a state of continual sorrow is quite unbearable.

Spiritualism and life after death is a subject which obsessed Peter Sellers and he relied heavily on well-known mediums such as Doris Collins and Maurice Woodruff to direct his life.

As a boy living in Ilfracombe, his best friend was Terry, the son of a medium, Estelle Roberts. Shortly after the Second World War Sellers went to see Estelle who, in mid conversation, turned away from him and asked, 'What did you say?' as though someone else was there. Then she questioned Peter about an uncle of his and asked if he had a picture of that uncle. As it happened, Sellers had a group photo in his wallet which included his uncle. Estelle picked the uncle out straight away.

'She was extraordinary,' he later told me. 'How could she have known? I'd never talked to anyone about my uncle.'

She told Peter, 'Nobody's dead. There are no dead people, just people living another parallel life with us. They have everything we have; they have gardens, and flowers, and food. They have whisky.'

During a time when he lived in Ireland with his third wife, Miranda, a hen they kept went missing. Miranda was so distressed that a fox might have got it that Sellers decided to hold a seance to contact his dead mother. He asked her, 'Do you know where the hen has gone?'

'Of course I do,' she replied through the medium. 'It's up in the rafters of the stable.'

'Hang on,' said Sellers, 'I'll take a look'. He could not find the hen and when he got back he told his mother, 'It's not there.'

'Of course it's there. Go and have another look. But don't be long. I'm not sodding about all night looking for a perishing hen.'

The following day he found his hen up in the rafters.

Doris Stokes seemed to have less luck contacting his mother. Said Spike Milligan, 'Every time he went to see Doris Stokes, he tried to get in touch with his mother, but instead he got in touch with his dog, Chussy, a little white-haired Maltese terrier, who said it was very happy.'

His obsession with the occult was not restricted by international frontiers. No matter which country he was in, he would phone either Maurice Woodruff, Doris Collins or Doris Stokes to get in contact with his mother. Sometimes Sellers would be in the middle of using Tarot cards while his valet would be on the phone to one of the mediums, relating messages from his departed mother. The phone calls often went on for hours.

What his mediums told him, he acted upon. Mid-way through the filming of *Ghost in the Noonday Sun*, Maurice Woodruff told Sellers that the name of his character, Scratch, was an ancient name for the Devil. Sellers told the director, Peter Medak, that because of this, the Devil was blighting the film, and he insisted there and then that the name be changed to Scratchy, despite the fact that a good portion of the film had been shot using the original name.

Much of the film was shot on a galleon in the Aegean, and Medak was driven up the wall when Sellers refused to work on certain days because Woodruff had told him, 'Today is not a good day for being near water.'

Sellers once predicted, 'I shall live till I'm 75 and will die in my sleep shortly after that. I know that. I suppose I knew all the time I would never die during that Hollywood business. But you have to watch things. Even so, I think I shall most probably die about then – 75 – that age.'

He was some 25 years out. His life on this earth ended in 1980 when he had a fatal heart attack in his suite at the Dorchester Hotel in London. Not long after, I went to see his widow, Lynne Frederick, at the Dorchester and found that she seemed to have come to terms with her loss remarkably well.

It transpired that, only a few days after Sellers's death, she had gone to the home of Michael Bentine to meet Doris Collins. Lynne was depressed and nervous when she arrived. Bentine and his wife left Lynne and Doris Collins alone for an hour, during which time Peter Sellers manifested himself. She told me, 'It was an extraordinarily moving experience but not sad. It was uplifting, so I didn't cry through it. And he hasn't lost his sense of humour.'

Lynne too is gone now, dying so young in 1995. Well, perhaps she is with him, enjoying his life-after-death sense of humour.

Not all who have sought contact with the dead have been so willing to accept what they saw or heard. Perhaps no other person has done so much to expose fraudulent mediums as Harry Houdini. He remains a legendary name in the art of illusion and escapology but what is largely forgotten is that he was also a film star.

He went into films because as he got older – and he was only 44 when he did in 1918 – he felt he could not go on hanging off skyscrapers in straitjackets for ever. He also needed a plentiful supply of money to maintain his large staff, so he signed to star in *The Master Mystery*, a serial which took six weeks to shoot in which he played a detective called Quentin Locke. The film, and his subsequent pictures, took full advantage of his ability to perform amazing stunts. But he shied away from screen romance. To him, a screen kiss was not something to be taken lightly and, unable to bring himself to do anything which might be regarded as being unfaithful to his beloved wife Bess, he refused to kiss his leading ladies. 'I'm afraid I'm not much of a ladies' man,' he told a Hollywood columnist. 'I am so old-fashioned that I have been in love with the same wife for 25 years.'

The Master Mystery was an enormous success and he was signed by Jesse Lasky who, with Adolph Zukor, had just formed Famous Players-Lasky. He began writing and producing his own films, and he and and Bess enjoyed living in Hollywood where they rented a bungalow. They were used to moving around the country all the time and they found that to stay in one place longer than a month was a novelty. Asked what his favourite holiday spot was, Houdini replied, 'Hollywood.'

It seemed they had arrived in town at the right time for someone so interested in Spiritualism. Movie stars everywhere were trying to contact the dead and there were plenty of mediums willing to take money from the wealthy stars to act as go-between twixt them and their dearly departed.

Bess had been born into a family which, she said, believed in 'ghosts, witches, and the power of the evil eye and supernatural evils'. When she first met Harry Houdini, he showed her how easy it was to fake mediumship by getting her to write the first name of her father, which she had never told him, on a piece of paper, crumple it up and burn it. He told her to rub the ashes onto his arm and her father's name, Gebhardt, appeared in blood-red letters.

It completely terrified her, until he showed her that he had in fact easily discovered her father's name, scratched it on his arm with a sharp instrument and, by rubbing it hard, made the letters show up in red. Later, before Houdini became active in medium-busting, they included Spiritualism in their act.

In 1913, Houdini's mother, to whom he was devoted, died. He became determined to find an authentic medium in order to contact her. In 1919 he took a break from Hollywood and visited England where he met noted author Sir Arthur Conan Doyle. Doyle and his wife, Jean, were confirmed Spiritualists and Jean practised as a medium. By this time Houdini had begun exposing fake mediums but this seemed not to concern the Doyles. In 1920, Houdini invited the Doyles to meet him and Bess in Atlantic City. There the Doyles asked Houdini to join them for a special seance to contact his mother.

Houdini later said, 'Sir Arthur started the seance with a devout prayer. I had made up my mind that I would be as religious as it was within my power to be and not at any time did I scoff at the ceremony. I excluded all earthly thoughts and gave my whole soul to the seance.'

A spirit was summoned and Lady Doyle asked, 'Do you believe in God?' Her hand rapped the table three times, which meant yes. Then she said, 'I will make the sign of the Cross,' and drew a cross on the edge of her paper pad. Then the spirit identified itself as Houdini's mother, and as she communed, so Lady Doyle wrote the words.

Houdini said of that experience, 'I was willing to believe, even wanted to believe. It was weird to me and with a beating heart I waited, hoping that I might feel once more the presence of my beloved mother. I especially wanted to speak to my mother because that day, 17 June, was her birthday.'

And yet the spirit had failed to mention that this was her birthday and Houdini felt the message he received was so generalized it meant nothing to him. He was also bothered that the message had been written in excellent English when his mother had never been able to write in English and spoke in broken English.

He also questioned the fact that his mother had begun the session with a sign of the Cross – she was an orthodox Jewess.

Given time to consider it, he concluded that no contact had been made with his mother although he conceded that the Doyles were sincere in their beliefs and he held them both 'in the highest esteem'. The Doyles took exception to this and their friendship waned.

As Houdini went from one medium to another, he became something of a crusader in exposing fakery, delivering anti-Spiritualist lectures and demonstrations, writing books and articles and making of himself an enemy to the cause of Spiritualism.

He became a member of the Scientific America committee which offered a prize to anyone who could prove genuine mediumship in 1922. Mina Crandon, a well-known Spiritualist who called herself Margery, took up the challenge. She claimed to be led by the spirit of her brother Walter, who had been killed in a train crash in 1911.

Over the next two years Margery impressed the committee in numerous sessions, but none of which Houdini was present at. He objected when the committee tried to award her the prize and he insisted he be present at further seances. But he imposed strict controls, designing a cabinet in which Margery could be enclosed with only her hands and head visible.

During a seance, a spirit seemed to ring a bell. Houdini discovered a folding ruler in the cabinet and accused Margery of smuggling it in to work the bell which was contained in a small box. She retaliated by saying Walter told her that Houdini had planted the incriminating evidence.

The battle between Margery and Houdini, who came to hate each other as the tests continued, rolled on into 1925, by which time Houdini had given up making films, his last being *Haldane of the Secret Service* in 1923. He was devoting much of his time now to medium-busting and Margery was his arch-villain. After many tests and much arguing, the committee decided against awarding her the prize.

Now Houdini was conducting his crusade against fake mediums with vigour and vengeful mediums predicted his death. Suddenly, in 1926, he did die, unexpectedly, on Halloween, from a ruptured appendix. One of his assistants claimed he had placed the ruler in Margery's cabinet on Houdini's orders. Some illusionists who knew Houdini believed that he may have framed her because he knew she was a fraud and had been unable to prove it.

Houdini had said, 'If it is possible for anyone to get through after death, that person is me.' A rumour spread that Houdini had prepared a message in code which he with his wife used in their stage act and which he would send from the other side. A number of mediums claimed they received his message but Bess refused to endorse any of them.

She found life difficult to cope with after Houdini's death and his failure to reappear. She began drinking and her money began to run out. She hoped to recoup some money from the box-office takings from his films which had earned big profits. But prints of his films had been widely shown without due care to copyright, and without proof of ownership Bess was unable to get back all that was due. She became ill, muddled and in despair.

In 1928 she received a letter from American medium Arthur Ford who claimed to have contacted Houdini. Bess endorsed his claim, but a newspaper reporter revealed that he overheard Bess and Ford conspiring to invent the story so as to make money on a special personal appearance tour.

Bess denied conspiring with Ford, saying she was ill and distraught, had been confused and frail, and found she was doing and saying things she should not have done. She also denied that there was a coded message but she did continue to hold seances on Halloween for several years to see if Houdini really would contact her. He never did.

She once said, 'There was a period when I was ill – really mentally ill as well as physically. I wanted so intensely to hear from Harry that Spiritualists were able to prey on my mind and make me believe they really had heard from him.'

Author Ruth Brandon, who wrote a biography of Houdini as well as a book called *The Spiritualist*, attended a Halloween seance at the Holiday Inn in New York where she and ten others sat around a table trying to raise Houdini. With the exception of Brandon, the rest of the group met every year for this event. Yet again, Houdini did not appear. However, there are mediums today who claim to reach him on Halloween. It's appropriate that one of his most popular films was *The Man from Beyond*.

Despite all I have heard about life after death, the story that impresses me most in its absolute conviction is that of Peter Cushing's 23-year mission to be reunited with his beloved wife Helen. It's a story that has nothing to do with seances and mediums. It's about a man's total conviction – about which he was extraordinarily matter-of-fact. And, perhaps suitably for a man whose films were concerned with the supernatural, his story culminated in a mystery.

Peter Cushing was something of an institution in the British

film industry throughout the 1950s and the following two
decades. He was not just a film actor but a major movie star.
Most of all he was one of the masters of horror – his only rivals,
though they were friends, were Christopher Lee, Boris Karloff
and Vincent Price. He never forsook Britain in favour of
Hollywood and, with Christopher Lee, was the mainstay of
Hammer Film Productions, *Dracula*, *The Curse of Frankenstein*,
The Mummy and many of the sequels.

He also played some excellent character roles, making a
perfect Sherlock Holmes in *The Hound of the Baskervilles* as well
as in a TV series, and proving his acting versatility in films like
Olivier's *Hamlet*, Samuel Bronston's *John Paul Jones* and George
Lucas's *Star Wars*.

He was a much satisfied man in his career and his home life.
He was married to Helen for 27 years. And when she died in
1971, it was as though his life had come to an end. He was so
devastated he retreated into solitude. Then he suddenly re-
emerged and threw himself so wholeheartedly into his work that
he made one film after another without a break. He continued to
work frantically, taking only a two-year break after *Star Wars* in
1977.

I recall hearing rumours during the early 1970s that he was a
sad man who was waiting to die. I discovered for myself that this
was not true. He was in fact a man joyfully looking forward to
joining his wife. The first inkling I had of this was when I
interviewed him at Pinewood Studios where he was making *At
the Earth's Core*. I happened to mention that making film after
film, as he was doing, must have made time pass very quickly.

'Oh, but my dear boy,' he said, 'that's the whole point.'

The next time I saw him was in 1980, on the set of *A Tale of
Two Cities*. He had aged considerably, he looked very frail and
was chain smoking, completely oblivious to the hazards to his
health at the age of 67. He looked at least ten years older.

He talked a lot about painting, which partly filled his time in
between films. He worked a lot less now, making about one film
a year. He did not think he was a particularly good painter. To
my surprise he said, 'I think when I start again, I'll become a

good painter.'

I asked, 'When you start what again, Peter?'

'The next time round. We all go off somewhere. It doesn't finish in this world, I'm sure. You know, Churchill believed this and he decided that he would paint for the first hundred years when he died. I firmly believe we were all put in this life to learn how to behave in the next.'

He also said, 'My dear Helen will be waiting for me and I don't want to keep her waiting much longer.' When I asked him how he knew, he replied, 'I just know it.'

He felt she was with him still. Whether or not he ever contacted her through a medium, he did not say. But you could tell that he felt her presence. He signed all his letters 'From Peter and Helen.' And if it was all in his mind, it did not matter because it eased his pain over the 23 years between her death and his. He said, 'When my dear wife was alive I had a reason to live and my life was fulfilled. Until the time comes when I can join her, I'll pay the bills and continue to work.'

And he did until his death in August 1994 from prostate cancer. His illness had first struck in 1982. He was admitted to hospital where doctors gave him 15 months to live. Fifteen months later he was well enough to go home. Cushing would have been disappointed that he had to wait a further 13 years to leave this life. All that time he was taken care of by his secretary and housekeeper, Joyce Broughton.

She nursed him and cared for him until he died. But shortly after his death, this great British movie star and fine actor became the subject of a mystery. His ashes were placed by the side of his wife's remains in the local church grounds in his home town of Whitstable, Kent. There was a headstone by Helen's grave, which had a space next to her name 'to allow for mine when that joyous day comes.'

But within a year of his death the headstone and his remains disappeared. The townsfolk, who were enormously fond of Cushing, were mystified and outraged. All that could be uncovered was that the local vicar had allowed Peter's ashes to be removed, insisting that he was actually following Peter's secret wishes which he imparted to Mrs Broughton. The location of his ashes was not to be made public.

This explanation did not satisfy the townsfolk because they had heard Peter say that he wanted to be left to rest at his wife's side in the town he loved. The vicar was unable to confirm or deny that Cushing's ashes had been removed from Whitstable altogether.

As for the removal of the headstone, Cushing had asked for it to be taken away because ghoulish tourists had written graffiti on it and Peter, who tended Helen's grave every day, had become increasingly upset by it.

So the whereabouts of Cushing's remains have become a mystery because Helen's ashes remain in the churchyard. I have my own theory. A good one, I think. Peter wanted to be with his wife. He never made any mystery about that. I do not think he would have allowed his remains to be removed from Helen's side. I think his remains have been placed with hers, fulfilling his wishes to be with his wife and to remain in Whitstable.

Wherever his remains are, and whether they are with Helen or not, I am convinced that at the moment of his passing, Peter Cushing was a happy man. Said film producer Kevin Francis, 'He'd be annoyed if we were sad. He has been waiting to join Helen for 23 years.'

Christopher Lee said, 'He couldn't wait to join Helen. Only now is he happy.'

5

Psychics of the Cinema

The problem with the paranormal is trying to figure out where one aspect of it ends and another begins. Take the following case for instance. Try to decide if it is a tale of near death experience, or one of a spirit from the other side, or an extraordinary example of an individual's own emotional, mental and even psychic ability to overcome disability and maybe even death.

Tommy Steele, who began as a rock'n'roll star, remains one of Britain's favourite entertainers. He made a few modest films like *Tommy the Toreador*, became a star of stage musicals in the West End and on Broadway with *Half a Sixpence*, went to Hollywood to star for Walt Disney in *The Happiest Millionaire*, and followed this by two more big screen musicals, *Half a Sixpence* and *Finian's Rainbow*.

But before all that fame and fortune was his, he was Tommy Hicks who ran away to sea at the age of 15. After serving only a short while on a merchant ship, he fell ill and had to be flown back to England and put in a London hospital. Spinal meningitis was diagnosed and his family were summoned to his bedside: he was fighting for his life.

By the following morning he was paralysed from the waist down and doctors ushered his family out to permit young Tommy to rest. Screens were placed around his bed.

In his semi-conscious state, he heard a child laughing. Suddenly a brightly coloured bouncing ball came over the screens and landed on his bed. He reached a hand towards the ball. It was almost out of his reach. He was weak and could feel nothing in his legs but he just managed to touch the ball and grasp it. He thought that the child would be expecting his ball back so, somehow finding the strength, Tommy tossed it back over the screens.

He lay back again exhausted and slipped again into semi-consciousness. But suddenly the ball came back, landing further down the bed. Mustering all his strength, he leaned forward, grabbed the ball and threw it over the screens. The ball came back.

Several times over the next hour Tommy threw the ball back, and each time it came back it landed just a few inches further away from him. Almost without noticing, and with each reach, he was getting stronger and managing to sit up more each time. He noticed the feeling was returning to his legs and before long he could move them.

When his doctor discovered the progress he had made in just an hour, they were amazed. His fever was passing and the paralysis was disappearing. Clearly, his condition was no longer critical but they could not understand what had cured him. So he told them that it was all due to the little boy who had made such a game of throwing the ball over the screens.

'What little boy?' one of the doctors asked him.

They pulled back the screens and Tommy saw there was no little boy in the room. Nor had there been. He described the ball that kept coming over the screens and this struck a chord with his parents. They said, 'Don't you remember? The ball is the one you gave to Rodney for Christmas.'

Rodney was Tommy's younger brother who had loved the ball he had been given. Not long after, Rodney died, aged just three.

It may be called an act of spiritual healing. But that usually involves a healer. In this case there was no one else present, except for a little boy who may or may not have been a spirit, and who may have been Tommy Steele's dead brother. Or it may have been that Tommy, in a semi-conscious delirium, experienced a state similar to NDE, or NDE itself. Or was it another kind of psychic experience, whereby he conjured up the vision to give him the will to survive? The possibilities become endless, and endlessly frustrating.

In the early days of Hollywood there were all sorts of mystics performing a variety of occult arts. Hollywood reporter Leo Rosten recalled one particular healer who practised his wonders by taking a drop of blood from each of his clients, instructing them that they should call him on the phone the moment they felt a headache or depression coming on. When a call for aid came, the healer bombarded the client's blood sample with 'health rays' which were produced by a 'power-giving' machine in his possession and which nobody ever saw. By this miraculous process, the health rays managed to reach the body of the client. Since a good many of his clients were also likely to be sniffing cocaine, smoking dope or consuming large quantities of alcohol, they never seemed to complain that their headaches or depression lasted long.

Psychic ability is, by its very nature, an inexplicable phenomenon. It's also incredibly common. Most people have experienced some form of Extra Sensory Perception, or made a prediction that came true, or were thinking of someone who phoned at that very moment. In a study carried out in Canada on 502 people in 1992, 17.8 per cent claimed to have had a dream which predicted a future event in some way and 15.6 per cent had experienced ESP at least once.

What that ability is and where it comes from is an age-old question, like every other aspect of the paranormal. What I have observed, though, is that a lot of actors seem to have psychic or ESP ability. Maybe it has something to do with the gift actors possess that enables them to tune in to a character in a film or a play and bring it to life; an extraordinary sensitivity that is the intangible part of acting, beyond all the techniques.

It's hard to believe Sophia Loren when she says, 'I'm a witch'. But she has said it, she has written it in her autobiography, and she believes it. Not that she implies that she flies on a broomstick or turns people into toads. It is a description she gives of herself because, she says, 'I have acute extra sensory perception.' Maybe that is exactly what the witches of old, who were burned at the stake, possessed.

She cites many instances of her ESP, such as the time when she and her film producer husband Carlo Ponti were staying at the Hampshire House in New York, and Ponti was recalled to Milan when his father died. He left Sophia, his sons Alex and Carlo Jr and their new baby, in the Hampshire House apartment.

At about nine o'clock that evening Sophia went to her room, only to become aware of a 'presence,' of a 'sinister black moving shadow' casting its shape across the room. She ran from the room and returned only when Alex came with her to investigate. They found no one there. Sophia said good night and went to bed.

She awoke in the early hours of the morning to find three armed robbers in the apartment. They had seen her being interviewed by David Frost on television and noticed that she wore a fabulous diamond ring. She tried to explain to them that the ring had in fact been loaned to her by Van Cleef & Arpels. One of the men hurled her to the floor and demanded to know where her baby was. Convinced her baby's life was in danger, she begged them to believe her when she said she did not have the ring. Fortunately one of the men decided that the other jewellery they had found would do and they left.

She was convinced that the shadow and the presence in her room earlier had been a premonition and she blamed herself for not heeding it. The cynic would argue that this was no premonition at all, that the shadow and the presence were just her imagination, and the fact that men came to rob her that very night was pure coincidence.

I might have thought so too. But Loren has had other experiences that make you wonder. Being particularly fond of candlelight, she often lights a candle in her living room. As a rule, her secretary extinguishes the candle before going to bed. One night in her Paris apartment, Sophia felt compelled to get out of bed and to return to the living room. She discovered that the candle was still burning. For the first and only time, her secretary had forgotten to put it out.

That in itself may not seem particularly important but, as she blew out the candle, she suddenly had a vision of a raging fire. It terrified her momentarily, but she put it out of her mind and went back to bed. Several hours later, she was awakened by cries of 'Fire!' The apartment block was ablaze. She and the family governess wrapped the children in blankets and went up to the roof where they were rescued by firemen. Sophia spent a day in hospital being treated for smoke inhalation.

She needed no convincing that the vision of fire had been a premonition.

On another occasion, she had 'an overwhelming feeling of impending disaster' shortly before she was due to fly from Rome to Brussels to attend a gala charity ball. This time she heeded the premonition and cancelled. The organizers felt put out at having their big star guest let them down, but they found a replacement, Marcella Mariani, a former Miss Italy and aspiring actress.

She travelled to Brussels on the plane Sophia would have caught and again back to Rome on the aeroplane that would have brought Loren back. Except, on the return journey the plane crashed. There were no survivors.

On another evening in Paris, Sophia and Carlo Ponti were in the middle of dinner when she asked if their Roman villa was insured against theft.

Ponti assured her that it was and asked her why she wanted to know. She replied, 'It's just something that has suddenly come into my mind.'

That evening their villa in Rome was broken into by thieves who stole a collection of antique boxes and Sophia's prized Oscar for her performance in *Two Women*.

As well as her ESP ability, she believes that she carries with her the spirit of her grandmother. 'When I need her, she is there. She is my guardian angel.' When she is troubled, she always speaks to her grandmother.

She says that if she had heeded more of her premonitions she could have avoided disasters like robberies and fires and adds, 'I shall never amount to much as a witch.'

Adam Bentine would never have described himself as a witch. But he was a much respected and experienced psychic, although he is better known as the father of Michael Bentine. Actor Jack Warner never quite believed Adam Bentine when he told Warner that he was going to become famous as a policeman.

Warner had appeared in numerous top British films, such as *The Captive Heart*, *Here Come the Huggetts* and its sequel *The Huggetts Abroad*. It may have seemed, at the time, a highly improbable prediction, but when Bentine looked at Warner, he saw him dressed in a policeman's uniform.

In 1950, not long after Bentine's prediction, Jack Warner was given the part of PC Dixon in the film *The Blue Lamp*. It hardly seemed like the fulfilment of Bentine's prediction for, as Warner told him, 'It's not the longest part I've ever had. I get shot in the first 20 minutes by Dirk Bogarde.'

Following *The Blue Lamp*, Warner played detectives in a few more films but never another policeman in uniform – not in a film, anyway. Still Adam Bentine maintained that Warner would become famous as an ordinary police constable. Then Ted Willis, who wrote *The Blue Lamp*, came up with an idea for a BBC TV series, *Dixon of Dock Green*, resurrecting the part of the ordinary PC the public had liked so much for Jack Warner. It ran and ran, throughout the rest of the 1950s, into the next decade, and into the 1970s. Jack Warner became the most famous TV policeman of his time, and everyone in Britain knew who he was.

Jack Warner had originally got to know Adam Bentine some years previously through another psychic experience. Bentine wanted to help his son Michael get started in show business and it was suggested that Jack Warner might be able to help. At the same time, someone suggested to Warner that Adam Bentine could help him with a very painful ankle that threatened to prevent him from going on stage in his own live show.

Warner phoned Adam Bentine and told him about the excruciating pain he was experiencing. Bentine told him that he would be healed during the night. Not knowing how this would happen, Warner went to bed that night in agony. At around three in the morning he awoke to the sensation of invisible but hot hands manipulating his ankle. The pain eased and he fell asleep. When he woke in the morning, the pain had gone and he was able to do his show that evening.

*

Michael Bentine has had some remarkable psychic experiences of his own. It seems he inherited his father's abilities and has seen ghosts, had premonitions and, as has been described previously, undergone a near death experience.

In the closing stages of the Second World War, he entered Germany as a member of Intelligence with the RAF. He says that the moment he crossed the border 'Germany stank of death'. He saw for himself the full horror of the death camps. To him it was a place of pure evil. 'Belsen hit us in the face with the foetid blast of Satanic darkness,' he said.

Around 1970 he returned to Germany to tour RAF bases. Driving along, one pitch black rainy night, he, his manager and another entertainer got completely lost. 'Then I felt it,' he later wrote. 'That awful creeping sense of evil.'

He told the others, 'We're near Belsen.'

They wanted to know how he could tell. 'I know,' he said. 'I can feel it.'

The car turned a corner and a hundred metres further on they came across Belsen. 'It still smelt of death,' said Bentine.

Following a concert, he got chatting to an Air Force chaplain and mentioned how he had felt the presence of the death camp. The chaplain told him, 'I'm not surprised. The whole area of the compound reeks of evil. No birds there. No bees either. The helicopter pilots say there is a downdraught over it. My dog won't go near it and neither will I. There is a psychic barrier around it.'

Bentine believes that paranormal phenomena are simply 'an extension of our natural awareness and mental abilities'. He believes we have three coexistent entities – the physical body, an astral body which is a linking medium and what he calls the 'Overmind, a complex, many-faceted entity that incorporates all the effects of the lesser entities.'

He says that death separates the body from the astral body which stays attached to the Overmind until that too separates. The Overmind is the sum total of our experience and heredity, existing 'in a parallel continuity to the universe of which we are a part'. There is a universal Overmind, which is God. For a fuller explanation, I recommend you read his book *The Door Marked Summer*.

In being able to predict the future, or what is commonly known as ESP, he believes that this is our own Overmind getting in touch with the universal Overmind. Among the events he has seen before they occurred was the American attempt to liberate the US embassy in Teheran where officials were being held hostage. He saw what he describes as 'a facsimile' of the disaster that awaited the American invasion force. He was in Spain at the time and wrote to a friend of his in the House of Commons to tell him about it, detailing the combined ground and air attack, the helicopters and the C-130 Hercules transport landing craft situated some 45 miles away from Teheran in the desert, and the disaster that would befall the force. It took five days for the letter to arrive but by the time it had, the failed mission had occurred the previous day.

During the war he found that he knew which of the pilots flying out would not return. If he looked at their faces and saw skulls, he knew those were the pilots who would die that night. The process was involuntary and he felt helpless since he knew that he could do nothing to prevent the pilots from going to their deaths. He became desperate to get rid of the manifestations and went to the chaplain to tell him what was happening.

He expected to be referred to the senior medical officer for psychiatric treatment. Instead the chaplain took Bentine into the small chapel and they knelt down and prayed for the manifestations to cease. They did.

Bette Davis never claimed to have ESP herself but she was convinced her mother had the gift and that if it were not for her mother, we never would have heard of Bette Davis. She related the following experience of her mother's ESP:

When I was only 18 years old I was with my mother and sister in Ogunquit, Maine, where a gypsy fortune teller told me, 'You will be known in every country in the world.' Of course she may have said that to everyone and was bound to get it right one time, but the strange thing is that it would never have come true if it were not for my mother's own clairvoyant gift.

Mother was very old fashioned even for her day. But one evening, after much persuasion from me, I was allowed to accept a date with a boy alone. He brought two friends with him, and they brought a number of bottles of liquor which they didn't tell my mother about. My young man and his friends were soon drunk and I was frantically trying to decide how to get away from them and not have to ride in the car with one of them driving drunk.

That evening Mother went to see a play and happened to sit next to a beau of mine, Dick Thomas, and during the middle of the third act she had this premonition that I was in trouble, and leaned over and asked him if he would drive immediately to the Bonnebunkport Hotel to collect me and bring me home.

Dick arrived and announced he was taking me home which relieved me because I was still in a dilemma as to how to get there. In the car, Dick told me that my Mother had sent him because she had had a premonition that something terrible was going to happen to me.

The next morning my escort from the night before came to see me. He was absolutely white and stone cold sober. He threw his arms around Mother and said, 'Thank God you sent for Bette last night. One of my friends drove the car home and completely smashed it up. Bette would most likely have been killed.'

Having a clairvoyant in the family can obviously be a useful thing. Robert Mitchum's son, Chris, who enjoyed a modest acting career of his own – he co-starred with John Wayne in *Big Jake* among other films – has a psychic ability which Dad takes full advantage of. Said Mitchum the elder, 'I always call Chris from the airport and tell him which flight I'm checked-in on. He can tell me whether the flight's going to be bumpy, whether it's going to arrive on time or be delayed. He's had bad "vibes" and that's good enough for me. I'm grateful for Chris's ability, whatever it is.'

Peter Sellers believed he had ESP. He said, 'It happens to me all the time. When I'm driving I can tell if a man is going to cross the road in front of me, even if he's nowhere in sight.'

The late Michael Landon, who had the rare experience of having three successful TV series in his lifetime – *Bonanza, Little House on the Prairie* and *Highway to Heaven* – believed he had extra sensory perception.

He once said, 'I have ESP ability and frankly it really scares my wife. I'll never forget the time I shocked her with it. She had bought me a birthday gift but refused to tell me what it was. Then one night lying in bed, I found myself gazing at the ceiling and I saw an image of the present – a watch. I described it perfectly, even the brand, and my wife was frightened. She begged me not to say another word.'

Sylvester Stallone is a believer in psychic powers, stemming no doubt from his famous mother's psychic abilities. He is sure that premonitions play a part in his life and have on occasions saved his life. He recalled how his former wife, Brigitte Nielsen, had a premonition that prevented a premature death for the star of *Rocky* and *Rambo*.

It happened when he was making *Rocky IV*, filming a scene in which Dolph Lundgren pummels him in the heart. Said Stallone, 'I'm getting paler and paler, and she has a premonition that I'm in trouble and that I must get to the hospital immediately. She kept at me until I finally gave in. I was in intensive care for nine days. A sac around my heart was very swollen, which is often fatal. So she was there for me at the right time.'

He had his own premonition another time but failed to act on it, putting his life in danger. He was filming a scene with Wesley Snipes for *Demolition Man* which involved a gun. Well, just about every scene in the film involved guns, but this one gave Stallone cause for concern. He said, 'I had an uneasy feeling throughout the scene. After the cameras had stopped rolling I checked the gun and fifteen shots spewed out. If things had gone wrong during that scene, it could have killed me.'

Italian film star Gina Lollobrigida was one of Sophia Loren's biggest competitors in the international film market. She was enormously successful during the 1950s in the American successes *Trapeze* and *Solomon and Sheba* but, unlike Loren, she did not manage to capitalize on her success in the 1960s. Nevertheless, La Lollo, as she was affectionately dubbed by the press, remains one of Italy's biggest movie stars, perhaps almost a movie legend.

However, like Loren, she has experienced the power of ESP, and recalled a strange experience she had as a little girl living in Subiaco, near Rome:

> Towards the end of World War Two it became a habit for my three sisters and me to sit in the window of our home and watch the American bombers on their way to targets in northern Italy and Germany. This evening we were all sitting near the window, eating, when my mother came into the room and said, 'You had better get away from the window. They are coming.' One of my sisters said, 'But they never bomb us.' At that moment a strange feeling came over me. It told me all was not well and that I should do something about it.
>
> I jumped up and told my sisters to get into the house and away from the window. They were about to protest but they saw I was serious, and we all moved away. A few seconds later a bomb exploded, shattering the window and the entire seat area where we had just been sitting. If I hadn't spoken, we would all have certainly been killed.

In 1979 a man named David Booth from Cincinnati informed the Federal Aviation Administration that he had experienced a series of dreams about a horrific air crash. He described the type of aircraft, its colour and the airline but did not know where and when the accident would occur. The details of his dream, however, proved accurate when, a week later, an airliner lost an engine as it was taking off from Chicago's O'Hare airport and crashed, killing all on board. Two passengers who had booked seats on that flight had cancelled. They were actress Lindsay Wagner and her mother. Wagner had also had a premonition about the flight.

Film stars have long been interested in all aspects of the occult and from the earliest days they were mesmerized by anyone with the ability. Some, like Basil Rathbone, claimed to have ESP. He was, wrote author William K Everson, 'the best all-round villain the movies ever had'. Born in South Africa in 1892, he became an actor when he moved to England, gaining a classical background performing Shakespeare before making his film debut in *The Fruitful Vine* in 1921. He went to the United States the following year and split his time between appearing in films in Hollywood and on stage in New York.

He was uneasy about being in Hollywood: 'It is a cruel place – relentless, stern and unforgiving – as I suppose all great industrial centres must be.' MGM signed him up to appear in *Reunion in Vienna* but he had a strong premonition that he should cancel the contract while there was still time and accept an offer to make films in Britain. MGM let him go and he made several films in Britain before MGM summoned him again to appear in *David Copperfield* in 1934. He played Mr Murdstone, a wonderfully loathsome character in which he gave a wonderfully loathsome performance.

He knew now that he was type-cast and for a while he went along with it. However, he also knew, he said, that he would soon break the mould and become a great hero. He was not sure who this hero was but he had a strong sense of something on the horizon and, in the meantime, he got on with his Hollywood career, waiting for it to happen.

In the interim he played Errol Flynn's arch villain in both *Captain Blood* and *The Adventures of Robin Hood*. Then, in 1938, his premonition came true – 20th Century-Fox invited him to play the Victorian super-sleuth, Sherlock Holmes, in *The Hound of the Baskervilles*. This, he said, was the chance he was waiting for: he made such an immediate impact that he became for evermore the definitive screen Sherlock Holmes in 14 subsequent films.

After the first Holmes film, he was able to slip easily between the roles of villain and detective with complete acceptance by the studios and audiences, breaking the type-cast mould. He had followed what he considered to be his psychic predictions, and earned himself a long and varied career that lasted until his death in 1967.

Japanese actor Sessue Hayakawa, best remembered perhaps for his portrayal of the Japanese camp commander in *The Bridge on the River Kwai*, yet active in Hollywood from the days of silent movies, amazed everybody with his ability to read unopened letters. It proved particularly useful when he received mail he preferred not to open. How he achieved this he never revealed and although some claimed it was just a simple trick, which it may well have been, he nevertheless insisted that he had real psychic ability.

Cliff Robertson had a similar experience long before he won an Oscar, for his role in *Charly* in 1969. I met him a few times but it was in 1979 on the set of a British-made chiller called *Dominique* that he told a remarkable story:

> I was raised by my grandmother who lived in La Jolla in California. So I was very close to her. When I was a young actor, I was performing in a play in New Hampshire some 3,000 miles from where my grandmother lived, and one night I had an extraordinary dream about my grandmother. She appeared to me and told me that her life was ending, and that I shouldn't grieve or be sad because she was ready to go and was at peace. I begged her not to go and she finally agreed that she would try to stay.
>
> I woke up in a sweat and checked the time: it was 3 am Eastern time. I had no phone to call my grandmother, which I felt desperate to do. I just paced about my room until around 6.30 am when a telegram arrived. It had been sent by an aunt in California who said that my grandmother had been taken ill at midnight. Midnight in California was 3 am in North Hampshire. My aunt said that my grandmother was not expected to survive and I was to fly

back to the West Coast immediately.

I had to go to the nearest town to find a phone, and I called La Jolla and found out that just after the telegram was sent, my grandmother had improved and was now past the critical stage and was getting better all the time. She surprised the doctor who was treating her who had expected her not to rally.

Jack Lemmon, though not experiencing ESP first-hand, had a similar tale to tell:

I was just 21 and going to college back east and had a close friend. We were playing tennis one afternoon when my pal was suddenly stricken with feelings of dizziness, nausea and most of all dread, all for no apparent reason.

I managed to get him home, and just as we arrived so did a man from Western Union with an emergency telegram. My pal read that his mother had died suddenly. She was some 2,000 miles away in the mid west. She hadn't been sick so her death was a complete shock. It turned out that she died at exactly the time my friend had suffered from those terrible feelings.

Vincent Price, one of the masters of horror, learned through a spectacular psychic experience that his friend Tyrone Power had died:

I was on a plane flying from Hollywood to New York, and I was reading a classic French novel. This was the 15 November 1958. I know it was the date because of what happened on that day. I glanced up to look out of the window and – I swear this is true – I saw huge letters emblazoned across a cloud bank which said TYRONE POWER IS DEAD.

It was a tremendous shock of course, and I thought that I was seeing things at first. I looked around and couldn't see anybody else acting as though they'd seen the words. But I had definitely seen these words which were like giant teletype that were lit up with brilliant light that came from within the clouds.

It was only when I landed in New York that I learned that my friend Tyrone Power had died in Spain where he was making *Solomon and Sheba*. He'd had a heart attack on the set while I was in the clouds. There was no way I could have known he was going to die so I didn't just imagine the words. Yet I think the words were somehow formed only for me, perhaps in my mind, like a message sent by Ty.

Sir Alec Guinness, one of Britain's great theatrical knights and star of countless films, is gifted with second sight. He predicted James Dean's death, and told him so. He met the young rebel star, who had just bought himself a Porsche, in Hollywood and told him, 'It is now ten o'clock, Friday the 23rd September, 1955. If you get in that car you will be found dead in it by this time next week'.

A week later, on 30 September, Dean was killed in that car. This was not an isolated incidence of Guinness's psychic power. He spent much of his childhood in boarding houses, one of which was haunted by 'an impoverished Miss Haversham'. More recently he has said, 'To this day I can still be apprehensive, on a grey day, when passing the shut door of a room I know to be empty.'

He once saw a painting he owned by Bernard Meninisky alter before his eyes. The trees and bushes in the painting began to move. The day it occurred was the anniversary of the artist's suicide.

Gloria Swanson, the great star of the silent screen and later immortalized in the Billy Wilder classic *Sunset Boulevard*, had a number of psychic experiences. When they first began, she found it difficult to accept that what she was experiencing was second sight. It occurred during the filming of Cecil B De Mille's *Male and Female* in 1919. De Mille moved his cast and crew to the uninhabited island of Santa Cruz off the Californian coast at Santa Barbara. One morning the company's Hawaiian propman, Johnny, went off in a small boat to run errands on the mainland.

By evening he had not returned and an assistant director became concerned for his safety.

Gloria Swanson told the assistant director, 'Don't worry, he's all right. He's with people who aren't Hawaiian.'

'What did you say?' the surprised assistant director asked.

Swanson was experiencing what she described as a 'flow of images,' and asked the assistant director, 'Is he a musician – because he's sitting at a piano.'

The assistant director said he did not think Johnny was a musician. Then Swanson announced that Johnny had stopped playing and was eating a bunch of radishes.

They both laughed and did not discuss it further. The following morning Johnny turned up safe and sound and, when Swanson and the assistant director heard Johnny's story, they were astonished to say the least. He had been to visit some Russians and had got there too late for dinner. But seeing they had a piano, he decided to sit down and 'plinked at the keys', even though he could not play. Then, feeling hungry, he went into the kitchen where all he found to eat were some radishes.

The particular form of ESP which Swanson experienced is known as 'remote viewing' – an ability to move one's perceptions virtually anywhere. Although she never learned to cultivate this particular gift, it is believed that remote viewers can actually see anywhere in space and time. As fantastic as this sounds, the CIA and other American Intelligence agencies have taken this very seriously and have been running a programme of remote viewing for the past two decades. Volunteer remote viewers have used their ability to discover the location of the most difficult Intelligence targets. It is considered a 'low cost radar system' by Intelligence agencies who also know that the Soviet Union had a similar programme running. They do not know how it works but because they have had success with it, they accept it.

I was once witness to a curious case of ESP *not* working. During the early summer of 1980, I went to the Athenaeum Hotel to interview lanky star James Coburn who was in London to talk about his film *The Baltimore Bullet*.

He sat in a chair, his head crowned with silver hair and the crevices in his face cracking wide when he gave that enormous grin of his. The phone in the room began to ring. He had been expecting his singing sweetheart Lynsey De Paul to join him there but she had not turned up. 'Maybe that's her,' I suggested as he picked up the phone. When he hung up he said, 'No, that wasn't her. She should be here later.'

Jim Coburn had long been intrigued by the mystical philosophies of the East and was interested in religions like Zen and Sufism. He had acupuncture to stabilize him when his mental and physical balance went awry, and he was given to banging his much celebrated gong because, he said, it relaxed him.

I asked if Lynsey was also into these things. He said, 'Her interests are in a different kind of field. She's interested in astrology and in life after death. She's also a little psychic.'

'Are you?' I asked.

'I'm not, but there is a certain synchronization that happens between us. When you're close with somebody you have that kind of synchronization. I look at her and say, "Shall we . . . ." and before she's heard what I'm going to say, she says, "Yeah," and we're off, knowing exactly where we're going without saying it. Or I've said, "Don't you think we should . . . ?" and she's said, "I've just done it."'

Apparently a clairvoyant once told Lynsey that she would go to America and meet the man of her dreams. She met Coburn at a party thrown by Joan Collins in Hollywood. (Sadly Coburn was not to be the man of her dreams as they later broke up.)

From time to time during our interview Jim seemed a little agitated that Lynsey had not turned up. He then spoke about something that in a way illustrates what I was saying earlier in this chapter, about actors being able to tune in to characters in films and plays that perhaps makes them more susceptible to ESP experiences. I had asked him if, being somehow psychically linked to Lynsey, he had ever found the same kind of things ever happened in his work. He said:

They happen all the time but I think of them as *accidents*, and when they do, I take advantage of it. Like when I was making *The Baltimore Bullet* in which I play Nick Casey, a pool hustler who goes from pool hall to pool hall, trying to make the $20,000 he needs to challenge the Deacon, played by Omar Sharif.

I am just an average pool player, but when I was Nick Casey I was suddenly playing great pool. They would set up pool shots for me that ordinarily I could never do, and I would get in there and I'd make those shots. Pretty soon I was knocking them all in, and they weren't just easy little putts. That was Nick Casey in there and just a little of me. A pure accident.

Towards the end of the interview Jim Coburn was in need of his gong because Lynsey had not turned up and he was growing restless. I turned off my tape recorder and he headed for the phone, this time to call her house.

When he hung up he grinned and told me, 'She's been at home all the time. She was expecting me there, and I thought she was coming here.'

For that one afternoon, James Coburn and Lynsey De Paul had gone out of synchronization.

6

Nothing to Fear But...!

Actors are so superstitious, generally speaking, that you never wish one luck before going on stage. Instead, you tell them to 'break a leg'. Now this may seem a rather unhappy blessing to pronounce but actors accept it with thanks, because to wish 'good luck' is tantamount to wishing disaster. This, apparently, stems from the ancient Greeks who considered that you should always conceal your true wishes from the gods, lest they thwart your desires. In essence, to wish an actor 'good luck' is tempting fate. So you let the gods hear you ask for something pretty horrible to happen, and telling an actor to break a leg should fool the gods who, after all these centuries, still have not caught on.

Actors can also get very funny about colours. Green is said to be bad luck, although it probably has more to do with the fact that green is a difficult colour to light properly and is therefore unpopular. Peter Sellers banned certain shades of green from his life completely. He said, 'The hard, acidy green is bad. I pick up strange vibrations from it. It disturbs me.'

During the filming of *After the Fox*, Italian director Vittorio de Sica told Peter Sellers that purple was 'the colour of death'. The director allowed no one to wear the colour around him. Sellers, who believed De Sica implicitly, promptly banned purple from his presence for ever. His secretaries had to check all visitors in case they were wearing the dreaded colour and those who were were shown out and told not to come back until they had changed their attire.

When Sellers was to appear in a restaurant scene in *Hoffman*, he discovered the tablecloths were purple and flatly refused work on the set: the cloths were changed to red ones. An enormously expensive set built for *Casino Royale* had to be torn down because he had had a nightmare in which his mother came on to the set and announced she did not like it.

Where does superstition end and the supernatural begin? Or are they one and the same? A good many people are superstitious about broken mirrors, walking under ladders, opening an umbrella indoors, or passing people on the stairs. See a ladder against a wall, most people will go around it. There is a good practical reason for doing so: there may be a decorator up there with a pot of paint waiting to fall on you. But I do not believe most people who avoid ladders are thinking that.

In the world of cinema and theatre, superstitions abound, often manifested by simple things, such as clothing or jewellery. Barbara Stanwyck always wore a gold medallion round her neck. It had to be removed for some films but she tried to keep it on if her costume allowed, or managed to conceal it out of sight. Fred Astaire believed that a particular plaid suit of his was especially lucky. Edward G Robinson carried an old silver dollar. John Garfield had a pair of old shoes which he insisted appeared somewhere in each film. Claude Rains wore an intaglio ring which he lost for two years. During that period every film he made flopped. He was overjoyed when he found it again and never took it off.

James Stewart always wore the same hat through his westerns of the 1950s and 1960s. He also rode the same horse whose name was Pie. When I interviewed him in 1979, I asked him why he had these preferences. He said:

> I felt the hat was a kinda good luck piece. It certainly got a good notice in the first picture! Actually better than I did! John Ford and I had a run-in at the very start of our first picture together, *Two Rode Together*, over that hat. He had a hat for me and I had this hat of mine, and we argued – and finally he let me wear the hat, but he said, 'If we ever do another picture together - which I *doubt* – I want you to have "hat approval" in your contract!'
>
> But he won out because on the next picture, *The Man Who Shot Liberty Valance*, I didn't wear a hat at all – on his orders.

And the horse, Pie – I had that horse for 20 years – amazing – yet never owned it because it belonged to a stunt girl who let me use it all those years. That horse had to be 27–28 years old – which is getting on for a horse.

The last picture I did with him was in Santa Fe, New Mexico, at an altitude of almost 6,000 feet. And it was just too much for ol' Pie. I couldn't use him. I had to use his double. And he died not long after. I don't know – the hat and the horse were just a quirk – a couple of good luck pieces.

I did some calculating and realized that Stewart's third film for Ford was *Cheyenne Autumn* in which the director made him wear a very smart white hat as opposed to his battered sweat-stained one. The film was Ford's most spectacular failure and virtually brought his career to an end.

As for the film which poor old Pie could not manage to do, it was *Bandolero*, in 1968. Straight after that Stewart made the comedy western *The Cheyenne Social Club*. It was a huge flop and Stewart has not made a western since, save for a fleeting cameo in *The Shootist*. So, for him at least, his hat and horse really were lucky talismans.

John Ford should not have complained to Stewart about his hat, because the grumpy old director himself wore what he thought was a lucky hat. In fact Ford had several lucky hats, so he, at least, had a choice to make each day.

Ford's favourite of all actors, John Wayne, insisted that he always used the same rifle and pistols in his westerns, and he always strapped on the same holster and nearly always managed to find at least one piece of clothing from a previous western to wear, whether it be a hat, or a shirt, or pants. And always – always – the same boots.

Aissa Wayne wrote in her memoir, *John Wayne, My Father*, 'My dad was deeply superstitious.' She said that he regarded a hat on a bed as a bad omen which would lead to a lack of work. When he saw a hat on a bed, he 'threw apoplectic fits'. And he cringed whenever his wife Pilar opened an umbrella indoors which she preferred to do before going out into the rain.

He loved to play poker but believed that a card which was accidentally turned face up was a terrible omen and he insisted that the player who dealt the upturned card should stand up and circle his chair three times. At the dinner table nobody was to ever hand him the salt for fear of handing him bad luck. The salt cellar had to be left in the centre of the table where he could reach it himself.

If he should be walking along the street with someone he loved, such as one of his children, and something physical came between them, such as a street lamp, he would utter 'Bread and butter'. He explained to Aissa, 'Anytime we have to walk around different sides of things, I have to say bread and butter. Or you do. Otherwise we'll stay divided.'

Superstition was part of what his 1964 film *Circus World* (known as *The Magnificent Showman* in the UK) was about. He played the owner of a circus who, ironically, spends much of the film trying to persuade the superstitious Claudia Cardinale that all forms of superstition are 'bunkum'. This meant that Wayne had to do things in the film that he would not dream of doing in real life. For one scene he had to throw his hat on a bed. He was anxious about doing the shot and told director Henry Hathaway, 'This could be a big mistake. The last thing we want on an expensive picture like this is bad luck.' But Hathaway persuaded him that the hat was just a prop and the bed was just a piece of set and nothing bad would happen.

In her book, *My Life with the Duke*, Pilar Wayne wrote that the film was 'a shining example of Murphy's Law. If anything could go wrong, it did.' As well as a series of minor accidents and script difficulties during filming in Spain in 1963, Wayne developed a hacking cough. Pilar begged him to see a doctor and he promised he would when filming was over. His cough got worse but it was almost a year later before he discovered he had lung cancer.

His co-star, Rita Hayworth, proved difficult to work with. Wayne was puzzled by her behaviour as he had known her for years and had looked forward to working with her for the first time. But she began arriving late on the set and did not know her lines. He and Pilar took Hayworth out one evening for a meal and after a glass or two of wine she seemed to lose control of herself, proving to be strangely belligerent. Wayne swore he would never work with her again.

Just when it seemed things could not get much worse, news came that President John F Kennedy had been assassinated. Wayne was not a huge admirer of Kennedy but the thought of the president's children losing their father made the Duke weep. And, of course, it was a stinging blow to someone like Wayne who was so passionately patriotic. 'We struggled to go on with our work,' wrote Pilar.

Then Wayne's young son, Ethan, was burnt at their Spanish villa when he sat on a heater. But the worst was to come. *Circus World* was the film that nearly ended the life of John Wayne. The spectacular climax to the film was the burning down of the big top. Wayne shunned the idea of using a stunt double and donned fireproof garments under his costume so he could be filmed close up to the flames. As the cameras turned he breathed in smoke which aggravated his cough. He came home after a day's filming on the fire, exhausted and unable to eat. Pilar begged him to get a stunt double, but he shrugged off the suggestion.

The next day he was back in the fire, hacking through the tent with an axe to create a fire break. As take succeeded take, the fire moved closer to him. Finally he could see nothing but smoke but did not know that the entire crew had been forced to abandon the set by the growing flames. He was waiting to hear Hathaway shout 'Cut!' but the director had fled with his crew. Wayne was choking and the flames were singeing his hair before he staggered out of the smoke to discover he was alone.

When he arrived home, he was barely able to catch his breath between violent bouts of coughing. He could not even manage to tell Pilar what had gone wrong and throughout he coughed up phlegm mingled with blood.

Pilar wrote that she 'couldn't wait to get away from the picture and the villa. Disaster seemed to cling to both of them.' The unit moved to London for some interior scenes. The cold, damp British weather made Wayne's cough even worse.

Finally, in September 1964, he was operated on for lung cancer. His left lung was completely removed.

The career of Wayne's co-star, Rita Hayworth, went steadily downhill, due to her health more than anything else. It turned out that during the filming of *Circus World* she was already in the early stages of Alzheimer's disease which took a firm hold on her during the mid 1970s and claimed her life in 1987.

As for the film, it was the last in a succession of expensive epics from independent producer Samuel Bronston, who had made *King of Kings*, *El Cid*, *The Fall of the Roman Empire* and *55 Days at Peking*. *Circus World* had to be a success. There was no room in Bronston's accounts books for a failure. But that's what his circus film was. Until then, no John Wayne film had been an unmitigated disaster. This one brought financial ruin upon Bronston and closed his studios.

It was, perhaps, the unluckiest film Wayne had ever made. And all because he threw a hat on a bed?

As well as keeping his wardrobe and props familiar on a film, Wayne also liked to surround himself with familiar actors. When he made what was to prove to be his last film, *The Shootist*, three years before his death from stomach cancer in 1979, he was literally surrounded with actors from his earlier films. The picture opened with a prologue that was virtually a résumé of his film career. He was in poor health when he made the film, but then he had been since 1964 when he had lung cancer. In the ensuing years he was short of breath and often needed oxygen, but this fact had been kept a secret from the public during his last 15 years. At the time *The Shootist* was made, there was no real reason to assume that it would be his last film. But Don Siegel, the director, seemed to feel the omens were predicting that this would be Wayne's last screen showdown. Siegel told me:

> I just knew it was going to be his last film. It had nothing to do with his health at the time, which wasn't good. And I'm not generally superstitious. But it was literally his whole

career coming together in one final picture, and I knew he'd never make another film. I mean, he was even playing a legend of the west who was dying of cancer. And that's what really got Wayne in the end.

The cast was made up largely of actors from Wayne's previous films. Lauren Bacall had been with him in *Blood Alley*. Richard Boone was in *The Alamo*. Hugh O'Brien was in *In Harm's Way*. John Carradine was in *Stagecoach*. Harry Morgan was General Grant to Wayne's General Sherman in *How the West Was Won*. And Duke's old friend Jimmy Stewart was in *The Man Who Shot Liberty Valance*. Even the music was by Elmer Bernstein who scored *The Comancheros*, *Big Jake*, *The Sons of Katie Elder* and *McQ*. It wasn't meant to be Wayne's last film; he didn't think it would be. But the omens were all pointing that way. And what happens? The film comes out in 1976 and nobody goes to see it. Wayne isn't bankable any more. The film looks destined to be forgotten. Then, suddenly, it's a classic. It's rediscovered. Now everyone says, 'Wayne's last film, *The Shootist*, is maybe the best western ever made.' Or one of the best. There's something really spooky about that picture.

Tallulah Bankhead, the gravel-voiced movie actress, was also a great star of the stage. During the 1920s she took Broadway in New York and the West End in London by storm with her titillating and extravagant performances. Before each performance she went through a ritual which she dared not break. She knelt before her gold-framed photograph in her dressing room, crossed herself and prayed, 'Dear God, don't let me make a fool of myself tonight.' Then she downed a glass of champagne and made her entrance.

She was mortified if anyone entered her dressing room left foot first. They would have to leave and return with the right. She also kept a rabbit's foot which her father had given to her. When she died in 1968, the rabbit's foot was buried with her.

Mrs Patrick Campbell was a leading British stage actress who made several films in the 1930s. (The 'Mrs' was part of her professional name, presumably to ensure everyone knew she was not a man.) She had a Pekinese called Moonbeam which she considered an essential good luck talisman. Moonbeam went everywhere with Mrs Campbell.

She never did quite learn to come to terms with stardom and its trappings and nonchalantly passed up all sorts of opportunities to make her a big star. In fact, she knew nothing about movies, and when she went to Hollywood to appear in several films she met the actor Joseph Schildkraut – who had been appearing in films since 1914 and made scores until his death in 1964 – and she told him, 'You are handsome enough to be in pictures.'

'But my name is Joseph Schildkraut,' he replied.

'Never mind. You can change it.'

By 1939 she had failed to cash in on her talent, mainly because she turned down every job that separated her from Moonbeam. When George Bernard Shaw asked her to star in the film version of *Major Barbara* that year, he told her it would be impossible for Moonbeam to accompany her. 'In that case,' she said, 'I shall have to refuse your offer.'

'But why?'

'Because Moonbeam is absolutely essential to my luck.'

She died a year later, at the age of 75, broke and all but forgotten.

Actors' superstitions often drove studio heads to distraction. Mary Astor believed that if the first day's filming went well, it was a bad omen. To ensure this did not occur, she gave less than her best on the first day. This must have been disheartening for directors who knew of her belief and apparently many of them made sure that she was not scheduled for the first day's filming.

Margaret Sullavan was said to refuse to start work on a film unless it was raining, which was not a very practical superstition in Hollywood where the sun shines most of the time. She had, in fact, a reputation for being one of the most difficult and temperamental Hollywood stars. She was insecure and neurotic and superstition seemed to support her neurosis. It did not help that in 1948 she was diagnosed as going deaf. She had to learn to act by lip reading but managed by and large to keep this secret.

In 1956 she walked out of rehearsals for a TV play, *The Pilot*, and straight into a private sanatorium in Massachusetts. In 1960 she said, 'I have a reputation of not wanting to go to work. I have never been what you call a dedicated actress.' Three weeks later she died from an overdose of sleeping pills.

Fridays were bad for Bessie Love who began her long career in 1915 in *The Birth of a Nation*. She never started a picture, travelled or made important decisions on Fridays. But because she was such a popular star, studios did not mind filming around her each Friday and she continued to be in work up to the time of her death in 1986.

Bruce Cabot was highly superstitious about the number 13. He had it stipulated in his contract that he never worked on the thirteenth day of each month.

Linda Hayden finds, like a good many actors, that she cannot help but be superstitious. She told me, 'Seeing a single magpie is very often a bad sign. When my father was very ill, a single magpie would come and religiously sit in our garden. My father died, and although I knew he would have died whatever happened, I can't help but associate it with seeing that magpie.'

Some superstitions are invented by actors because a certain chain of events is set in motion which they dare not break for fear of breaking whatever spell is seemingly cast. The 'Gypsy Robe' is a prime example. In 1950, a hopeful song-and-dance girl, a Broadway 'gypsy' – Florence Baum – landed a plum job in the chorus of the Broadway hit *Gentlemen Prefer Blondes*. She owned a tacky white satin gown, trimmed with feathers which had seen better days, and when another member of the chorus, Bill Bradley, asked to borrow it to use as a practical joke, Florence gave it to him.

He sent it to a friend who was just about to open in *Call Me Madam*, the new Ethel Merman musical. Bradley told his friend that the robe had belonged to one of Florence Ziegfeld's beautiful chorus girls and was known to bring luck to new shows. *Call Me Madam* turned out to be a huge success and, to show her appreciation for the good luck charm, Ethel Merman had a cabbage rose from her own costume attached to the robe. The legend of the Gypsy Robe had begun.

It was passed on to another dancer in the chorus of *Guys and Dolls* and that show was also a spectacular hit. Thereafter it became a much-needed talisman for every new Broadway musical and, with each show, chorus members who possessed it for the duration added new rituals. Each time it was passed on, it had to be delivered exactly half an hour before curtain up to the senior chorus member. Then the wearer had to twirl three times on stage before the show and every member of the cast had to touch it.

The wearer also had to visit each dressing room and every cast member had to sign it before it was passed on to the next show. New mementoes were sewn to it until, in 1954, it was too well worn to continue. So it was retired and a new Gypsy Robe was immediately put in its place for fear of breaking the run of luck that went with it to each show.

When a revival of *My Fair Lady* hit Broadway, the robe arrived three days late. The show, always a box-office hit, closed prematurely.

As Roosevelt said, 'The only thing we have to fear is fear itself.' Perhaps the cast of that revival were so fearful of failing without their talisman that they performed less than well and managed to turn a proven success into a failure. Fear, even when it is knowingly unfounded, can be a powerful force. Jenny Agutter told me that when she was making *An American Werewolf In London*, she experienced some frightening moments on and off the set:

> Doing this film I had a lot of bizarre dreams. Dreams about deaths in strange places, ghosts wandering down corridors, feeling as though I wasn't there but had become a ghost. I think it was all provoked by a state of mind because for any film that you're making you put yourself into the right frame of mind. It's like telling ghost stories when you laugh along with everybody, but you go back to your room

afterwards and you try to go to sleep, and it all plays on your mind. The same thing happens on a film set. You know that it's not real yet you try to evoke it and scare people, so therefore it does stay with you, which is why I think you hear all these stories about strange things happening on sets of horror films. People create that atmosphere.

If you're up after three in the morning, your mind is in a funny state and it all starts to become unreal. We were shooting down Clink Street in London, and at that time the whole thing became very frightening. You really were looking at shadows, wondering what was going on and hearing things. But it was purely your imagination running away with you.

I recall having lunch at Elstree Studios with a group of people including actress Caroline Munro when the subject of the paranormal came up. She said that a scene for *Dracula AD 72* was filmed in a church in which she was in a group of people trying to invoke the Devil or, as it happened, Count Dracula in the persona of Christopher Lee. She said that the cross was turned upside down, and from then on there was a peculiar atmosphere in the church, especially when the words of invocation were given. Nothing terrible happened but she said there was a definite feeling of something strange that unnerved her.

Down in Devon on the set of the thriller *The Shout* in 1978, I talked to the stars about the topic of the film which suggests that a man may be able to kill with just a shout.

'*The Shout* is really about superstition,' said John Hurt, one of the stars of the film. 'If you believe in superstition things will happen. Then it ceases to be a superstition. If you believe that something can kill you by supernatural means, it will kill you. And we know it is true, not just from the aboriginal societies who do believe they can kill with a shout but from other societies as well.'

His fellow cast-member Alan Bates concurred: 'I think this film is about the power of imagination. If you're serious enough and you believe it in enough, the power of that belief and faith can prove positive.'

I found a perfect story to illustrate this. A seventeenth-century French actor, Champmesle, had a recurring nightmare in which he saw his dead mother beckoning to him. He interpreted the dream as a forecast of his own death. He was no longer a young man, yet there was nothing about his physical condition to suggest he was at death's door. His physician examined him and told him he had years more to live. But Champmesle believed his death was imminent.

He booked a local church for his funeral, arranged for flowers, and organized a hearse and mourners. On the day of his burial, he turned up very much alive and well, and sat amongst his friends and family for his own funeral mass.

At the end of the service he thanked the priest, made his farewells to those who had come to see him off, and promptly died of a heart attack.

Is the point of believing a prediction will come true the point where superstition becomes the supernatural or where superstition becomes reality through the power of one's own imagination, sometimes through one's own fear? I realize I am treading on dangerous ground but when it comes to the subject of astrology, many people believe it has nothing to do with superstition. But there are those who allow their lives to be ruled by astrology and the fear of failing to adhere to what the stars advise surely borders on superstition.

Whether or not astrology is an accurate craft, or art or however its exponents may wish to describe it, is an on-going debate. There have always been plenty of people in the entertainment world who turn to astrologers to guide their lives. Douglas Fairbanks and Mary Pickford insisted on having their horoscopes presented to them daily, although it was Pickford who leaned more towards this belief. She planned her day according to her horoscope.

The omens were not good for Fairbanks and Pickford when they were cast together for the first time, by public demand, in *The Taming of the Shrew* in 1929. It seemed to United Artists that the film was a sure-fire hit. Fairbanks and Pickford were

Hollywood's royal couple. Everything they did turned to gold. But the stars – the ones in the heavens – foretold disaster and Pickford was reluctant to do it. In the end, she had no choice; Fairbanks, Joseph Schenck who was president of United Artists, and director Sam Taylor, had agreed on the project before Pickford was properly consulted.

On the set Fairbanks was, by all accounts, a complete cad who was irresponsible in his work and cruel towards Pickford. He did not learn his lines and he demeaned Mary who later said, 'My confidence was completely shattered and I was never again at ease before the camera or microphone.'

This early talkie was also filmed silent, just in case the new fad for talkies did not take off. The sound version was released and was a resounding failure critically and commercially. Mary Pickford was her own harshest critic, knowing that she had given the worst performance of her career.

Miriam Hopkins, star of silent films and early talkies, was another believer in various forms of fortune telling. She could read palms and cards and usually did at parties. She relied greatly on psychic advisers who worked on their predictions using numerology. That way she chose or rejected scripts, and avoided locations, addresses and hotel rooms.

Ida Lupino got caught up in the fad for astrology. Born in London and trained at RADA, she went to Hollywood in 1934 after several British films and became a star at Warner Brothers, usually playing hardened, often ambitious women. But in 1940, her first year at Warners, her belief in the heavenly stars caused chaos. She was due to star in *They Drive by Night* with George Raft, Ann Sheridan and Humphrey Bogart. But her astrologer predicted that the film would be bad luck. Consequently she announced that she would not report for work.

Director Raoul Walsh managed to film around her but, when he could no longer work without her, the film had to be shut down. The cast and crew were put to work elsewhere while Jack Warner, head of the studio, battled it out with her.

Eventually, she was forced to work and the film was completed and did well. Warner forgave her and put her opposite Bogart in

High Sierra immediately afterwards.

Through Mary Astor's father, John Barrymore, met theosophist Harry Hotchener and his wife, Helios. Helios was a student of East Indian philosophy and an astrologer. Hotchener became Barrymore's business manager for about ten years while Helios became Barrymore's personal astrologer. She drew up a chart for him every time he had an important decision to make.

There were believers and practitioners too among the film directors. Ernst Lubitsch checked his future on a daily basis through numerologist Mrs Thomas Platt. William Dieterle had the advantage of being married to a woman who had powers of prediction upon which Dieterle relied heavily. Charlotte Dieterle worked out the exact times that her husband's films should begin filming and when they should end, and Dieterle scheduled his productions to suit these requirements. For instance, Charlotte worked out that the filming of *Dr Socrates* had to begin shooting precisely at 9.02 on the morning of 6 June 1935. And it had to finish at 5.20 pm on 15 July.

When she deemed that filming on *Juarez* should start weeks before the studio was ready, Dieterle filmed an insert shot ahead of the regular schedule, just so that he would be sure of meeting his wife's psychic timetable. But she made life difficult for all concerned on that film because she decided that the title was particularly lucky since it contained six letters, and she insisted that no one should utter any other six-letter word on the set and so break the magic. Not surprisingly, some members of the crew thought she was off her head. But William Dieterle issued the relevant orders throughout the unit and, instead of issuing the usual commands, 'Camera!' and 'Action!' he began every shot with the words, 'Here we go.'

Numbers played an important part in the work of directors Anatole Litvak and Mervyn LeRoy. Litvak liked to have a staircase with 13 steps in each picture and LeRoy made every attempt to present the number 62 on the screen at some point in his films.

Many astrologers and numerologists made a good living in Hollywood – Carroll Righter, Myra Kingsley, Blanca Holmes and Norvell all had considerable power because their clients, from actors to studio heads, made important decisions based on their predictions.

New York astrologer Nella Webb served numerous film stars, notably Marie Dressler who rang Webb several times each week to find out what the stars had in store for her.

One of Hollywood's current superstar astrologers is Jacqueline Stallone, Sylvester Stallone's psychic mother. When Sly announced he was marrying Norwegian beauty Brigitte Nielsen, Mama Stallone predicted it would all end in disaster. She said, 'I could see it in the stars. He's Cancer, a water sign ruled by the moon, and so is she. He was born on July 6, 1946 and her birthday's July 15, 1962. I don't think people born under the same sign should marry, although I know some of the other astrologers don't agree – especially if they're both governed by the moon. They're just too sensitive, emotional and impractical.'

When she was asked if Sylvester believed her prediction would come true, she replied, 'He knew it would – but he didn't care! And that was the only time he hasn't listened to me.'

There was a time when Sir Alec Guinness consulted Tarot cards. He gave it up when he saw that the Tarot's symbols – the chalice, spear, tree and spiky crown – were all symbols of Christ's Crucifixion. Outraged by this blasphemy, he apparently threw the cards on the fire and shortly after converted to Catholicism.

An interest in astrology is, like superstition, common among actors. Diane Cilento, the Australian-born actress who starred in *The Agony and the Ecstasy*, *Hombre* and *Tom Jones* (and is, of course, the former Mrs Sean Connery), became interested enough to learn how to do it. She told me:

I have studied it a bit. I know how to work within a femeris and do charts. But I don't do them very often. I think one of the problems is there is hardly anybody who actually really knows what trians and quadians and those things mean. They can see that there is a thing where we say that the sun is in Aries and the moon somewhere else, but nobody knows exactly what that means. We've lost the art of it a long time ago. They can make up a lot of things and some things are handed down. It isn't a precise art, a precise skill at all. And it hasn't been considered as such since something like ancient times.

I think if you have the possibility of marrying intuition with knowledge, you could probably get to a pretty fair approximation of what the truth would be. But I don't think it is by any means infallible. We're all given to looking in the papers and reading our horoscopes, but we forget it by the next day.

Diane's words remind me of a friend whom I had not seen for several years and who, it turned out, has a set of Tarot cards. He did them for me and I was impressed by how uncannily accurate he was. I thought that maybe he had a great gift but he told me that although he could interpret the cards, he did not believe in them himself. A few years later he did them for a friend of mine whom he had never met before and, again, he was uncannily correct in what he said. But he still maintained he did not believe it himself. Perhaps that is the marrying of intuition with knowledge.

I once had tea at the BBC with British actress Mary Tamm who has appeared in many films, such as *The Odessa File*, although she may be better remembered as one of the celebrated female assistants in the BBC TV series *Dr Who*. That's what she was working on when I met her. Since she played a time-travelling, galactic-hopping heroine, it seemed only natural that we touch on the subject of astrology. Our conversation went like this:

MARY: I used to be more interested in astrology a couple of years ago. It was almost like a religion, and I virtually governed my life by it. Like I used to read every horoscope in every paper every day. Now it doesn't worry me if I don't. I do believe in it, but I certainly wouldn't lead my life by it like I used to.
ME: When did you become interested in astrology?
MARY: I started studying it when I was about twelve, and it

seems like I've read every book on the subject that's ever been written. When I meet people I still try and work out what sign they are.

ME: Have you worked out mine?

MARY: No, I haven't yet. I'll probably tell you later. I can always get people who are my own sign.

ME: What's that?

MARY: Aries. And I can always get Scorpios. You're not a Scorpio.

ME: No.

MARY: No, I didn't think you were. Those two signs I know very well. My sister is a Scorpio and so is a close friend of mine, so I always know Aries and Scorpio. It's often just a remark that gives it away. I can usually divide people into earth, air, fire and water – the four elements – and then you can usually pin them down. Are you Cancer?

ME: No.

MARY: I'll guess later. I really need an evening with someone to tell, and since I'm doing most of the talking, I'll make a wild guess later.

ME: Okay. But can reading horoscopes really affect your life?

MARY: A lot of it is autosuggestion, because if you read a horoscope and it warns you not to do something on a particular day and you don't do that thing and nothing awful happens to you, you think, ah, well, it must be right – I didn't have an accident because I was careful. I think those daily horoscopes aren't accurate anyway because you've really got to have your whole chart done to get an accurate analysis about what your character is like. I did see an astrologer who foretold something to me – meeting my husband. I saw a clairvoyant who told me through the Tarot cards I would meet my husband. That interests me more than astrology because astrology is now being proven to be a science whereas the psychic thing is something more interesting because it's inexplicable, and in my case it proved very true – everything that's been predicted has proved stunningly accurate.

ME: Are you psychic?

MARY: I am psychic in certain ways. I get dreams sometimes that foretell the future, or sometimes I can be thinking about someone and they ring up. But I've never had anything as major as knowing about a major event happening in my life. But I've been told I can cultivate my mind to do those things. I've got it. You're a Libra.

She was right.

7

The Accursed of Hollywood

If belief in superstition breeds fear and the fear of that superstition proves so strong that your own imagination can take over and thus create the very thing you are afraid of, could that constitute a curse? Is that what ultimately killed Jayne Mansfield? Was there something that was really devilish behind her death?

Jayne Mansfield had only one real ambition in life – to be a movie star. Becoming a better actress interested her little. So instead of trying to improve her acting ability and seeking better quality films, she spent much of her time courting publicity. She thought nothing of turning up at a press call for Sophia Loren, leaning over the Italian star and allowing her enormous breasts to fall out for the benefit of the world's cameramen. To say she upstaged Loren is to put it mildly. Mansfield knew her bosom was her greatest asset. *Variety* noted that she always looked as though she was leaning out of a window. She seemed destined for a life that delighted the editors of the scandal rags *Confidential* and *National Enquirer*. She was married at sixteen and a mother at seventeen. With her 40-18-36 figure, she won beauty contests and, during the mid 1950s, landed some TV walk-on jobs. When she appeared with her cleavage on show at the première of the Jane Russell movie, *Underworld*, the photographers had a field day, and the resulting publicity led to a contract for her with Warner Brothers.

Her early films were fairly forgettable but she scored a success on the New York stage in *Will Success Spoil Rock Hunter*, leading to a seven-year contract with 20th Century-Fox who were looking for someone to replace Marilyn Monroe. She enjoyed being a movie star, cared little about being a good actress and continued to court publicity. In fact, no one else knew how to get their face – and figure – into the newspapers like Jayne Mansfield.

When a reporter friendly with Jayne persuaded her to go along to San Francisco's Church of Satan to offer herself as a high priestess, she happily obliged. It would make for great photos: Jayne and the High Priest of Satan. This was in 1966, the year the Church of Satan was legally recognized.

Her new lawyer boyfriend, Sam Brody (she was estranged from second husband Mickey Hargity), thought it all a joke as he and Jayne toured through the church apartments. He scoffed when High Priest Anton La Vey hung a charm around Jayne's neck and bestowed an honorary title on her. Jayne, it seems, was not as flippant as Brody and was both wary and respectful of La Vey. But when the high priest became more amorous towards his honorary high priestess, Brody stopped laughing.

When they got to the Black Mass altar room, Brody was in a temper and, to spite La Vey, he lit some forbidden candles on the altar.

La Vey cursed Brody, telling him, 'You will be dead within a year.' Then La Vey told Jayne, 'This is serious. The Devil has cursed Sam Brody. He will be killed. There will be car crashes. Not one, but many. You must get out of his life or you too will suffer what he suffers.'

The ensuing newspaper stories alienated many of her fans. What concerned Jayne more was the curse. She gave May Mann, who was writing her biography, a series of interviews and talked about the curse. Mann told Michael Feeney Callan for his later book on Mansfield, 'Jayne was very serious and very scared. She felt certain something would happen and she didn't know how to avert it.'

Despite her fear, Jayne was drawn into La Vey's religion. Occult expert Eric Ericson wrote in his book *The World, the Flesh, the Devil*, 'Jayne attended the Friday rituals of the inner-most circle for acts of worship performed over the naked body of a woman as altar. Though it cannot be certain, it would be very much in character if [Jayne] volunteered herself as the altar.'

Despite La Vey's warning to get out of Brody's life, she stayed with him. When Brody drove his car, he drove fast. He managed to crash his car seven times in the six months following the curse, but none was too serious. In time Jayne seemed less concerned with the curse than she was with trying to survive a relationship in which her lover beat her, often in front of witnesses. One of his beatings nearly broke her back. She became more frightened of him than of La Vey's curse but, like so many battered women, she felt powerless to leave him.

Just before Christmas 1966, her son, Zoltan, was mauled by a lion at the Jungleland Zoo in the San Fernando Valley and rushed to hospital where surgeons fought to rebuilt his fractured skull. Jayne remembered the curse and said, 'It's a bad time, and it's not getting better.'

Just as Zoltan seemed over the worst, he was struck with meningitis. At the same time, Jayne came down with viral pneumonia.

The following year saw no let-up in her ill fortune. When La Vey called to see her, she seemed delighted but she was eager to placate him and his curse. She told her maid, Linda Murdick, 'I don't believe in this sort of thing, but you can't get away from the facts.'

Once, after she had allowed La Vey to use their pool for publicity photographs, she and Brody took him out for supper at La Scala where she brought up the subject of the curse. La Vey explained that once a Satanic curse was called down, it was irreversible. Brody laughed.

They dropped La Vey at his hotel and, on their way back home, they were involved in another car crash. They were lucky to walk away from this one, but their car was a write-off. Jayne told May Mann, 'I'm so tired from hurting all over from all these accidents. This curse just goes on working. Where will it all end?'

Her private life was in turmoil as Brody's violent behaviour and court battles over custody of her difficult teenage daughter Jayne-Marie continued. An uncle of Paul Mansfield, Jayne's first husband, wanted to become Jayne-Marie's legal guardian because, he said, Jayne was not a fit mother. Jayne-Marie claimed that Brody had beaten her and that her mother had allowed it. The uncle won the battle.

During the court case, Brody crashed his car for the ninth time. Jayne suffered some minor cuts but Brody broke an arm and a leg. When Jayne urged him to get La Vey to lift the curse, Brody just laughed. He still did not believe in the so-called curse.

By June things had calmed down a bit and she and Brody seemed to be happier. Jayne prepared to head off for Biloxi, Mississippi, where she was to perform at the Gus Stevens Supper Club. May Mann was with her the night before she left. Said Mann, 'She was restless and strange and she wanted to keep me up all night. We talked till 2.30 in the moonlight and she wanted to give me all these pictures and then she wanted to write down all her jewellery, like she was trying to put her affairs in order. I said I wanted to go home, but she pleaded with me. She was worried. She had a premonition. I saw it in everything she said.'

On the night of 28 June, having finished her stint at the club in Biloxi, she and Brody loaded their three children and Chihuahua dog Pupu into a Buick and headed for New Orleans, where Jayne was scheduled to appear on *The Midday Show* on TV the following morning.

Their driver was Ronnie Harrison, a 19-year employee from the club in Biloxi. Jayne sat next to him and Brody sat the other side of her. The children and dog were in the back.

By 2.30 am they were cruising along Route 90 with only 15 miles to go. Ahead a heavy lorry was moving slowly. The Buick, going much faster, ploughed into the back of it. Jayne, Brody and Harrison were all thrown from the car and died. Jayne was decapitated. She was just 34. The tiny dog was also thrown and landed dead near Jayne's headless body. The children, lying asleep in the back seat, survived.

Anton La Vey's curse, it seemed, had come true – to the letter. The thing is, was the tragedy avoidable, or were Mansfield and Brody on a course they could not get off?

Since James Dean crashed his silver Porsche in 1955, a trail of tragedy has followed which has been attributed rightly or wrongly to a curse. In 1971, one of Dean's former girlfriends, actress Pier Angeli, killed herself with an overdose of barbiturates. In 1976 Sal Mineo, who co-starred with Dean in *Rebel Without a Cause*, was stabbed to death just outside his Hollywood home. Another of that film's stars, Natalie Wood, died when she fell from her yacht and drowned in the waters off Santa Catalina Island in 1981. In 1985, Rock Hudson, who starred with Dean in *Giant*, died of AIDS.

Producer Roland Jon Emr was stabbed to death in 1991 while in the midst of putting together a biographical film on Dean. That same year the Dean family were sued by Warner Brothers for $30 million; the studio claimed they owned the rights to all James Dean merchandising. But in 1992, a federal judge threw the Warner Brothers' lawsuit out of court. Then Curtis Management Company, who represented the Dean family, sued Warner Brothers for $100 million, claiming that James Dean underwear marketed by Warners 'demeaned, degraded, diluted and diminished the value of James Dean's rights of publicity and trademarks'. Whether all these can be attributed to a curse or just happen to be a series of related incidents is up for speculation but what does have the ring of supernatural truth to it is the curse that is said to hang over the silver Porsche in which James Dean died and in which Alec Guinness had 'seen' his death.

Following the fatal crash, the mangled car was towed to a garage. It was decided that the car was beyond repair and should be broken up for spare parts. As the garage owner was working on taking the Porsche apart, the engine fell from its mountings and crushed him to death.

The shell of the car was restored and exhibited on a tour of the southern states of America. It was towed on the back of a trailer and proved an enormous though ghoulish attraction. Several times the truck pulling it crashed.

Meanwhile, parts from the engine were later purchased by a racing enthusiast who installed them in a hot-rod he was building. Another amateur enthusiast, a doctor, also bought spare parts from James Dean's famous Porsche and he too built them into a hot-rod. They both entered the same race. Both crashed, and both were killed.

The tour of James Dean's death car continued, as did the jinx. In Memphis, the car fell from its display mountings, landing on a teenager and breaking his hip. In Oregon the car inexplicably slid down its ramp and ran over three people, seriously injuring them. The tour came to an end in 1959 when the car somehow fell from its mountings one last time and broke up into almost a dozen pieces.

Another cursed Hollywood mode of transport was the yacht *Joyita*. It was built in 1931 by the Wilmington Boat Works in Los Angeles, by the commission of film director Roland West.

West had started out as a stage actor but began his Hollywood career as a director in 1918 with *De Luxe Annie*. He became highly regarded for his atmospheric films, some of which he also produced. In 1931 he became one of Hollywood's top directors with *The Bat Whispers*, a sequel to his highly successful tale of horror *The Bat*, made in 1926.

He married actress Jewel Carmen, but she was never really very popular with audiences and by 1931 she was a fading star. Having decided that, as a top producer-director, he ought to establish his status in the industry by owning his own yacht, he had one built, calling it *Joyita*, Spanish for a 'little jewel', in honour of his wife.

It was an ocean-going yacht, with a sturdy two-inch cedar planking and oak-framed hull. It was 69 feet long with a 17-foot beam, and a draft of 7 feet 6 inches. It was luxuriously equipped with the latest navigational aids, twin diesels, an automatic pilot, deep freeze and swivel chairs for deep-sea fishing.

But before it was launched West's marriage broke up. He began an affair with blonde actress Thelma Todd. She became the first lady of the yacht, and kept many of her perfumes and toiletries on board in her own suite.

The year the yacht was launched, West made *Corsair* and then spent the rest of his energies operating a road-side café in partnership with Todd. In 1932, however, she married Pat DiCicco, a member of the Mafia and Lucky Luciano's

Hollywood contact. West continued to live in an apartment over the café and maintained his relationship with Thelma but it all went from bad to worse when she began an affair with Luciano himself.

Luciano began putting pressure on West and Todd to allow him to use the upstairs of their café to run an illegal casino. When Todd threatened to 'spill the beans' on Luciano, he had her murdered in 1935. (The full story is to be found in my book *The Hollywood Connection*.)

In the ensuing cover-up in which Todd's death was left officially unsolved, West became a suspect and Hollywood turned its back on him. He never worked again. His bad luck had begun in 1931 just before his yacht was launched.

He sold *Joyita* to a man called Milton E Bacon who discovered that Todd's perfume bottles and toiletries were still on board. No one associated the yacht with any curse at that time, attributing West's bad luck to his own actions. The United States Navy commissioned the yacht for patrolling during the Second World War. In 1943 it ran aground off the Hawaiian Islands. Most of the lower part of the hull had to be replanked.

Joyita passed through numerous hands before being bought by Dr Ellen Katherine Luomala, an anthropologist at the University of Hawaii in Honolulu in 1953 – a year after Roland West's death at the age of 65.

Almost immediately the yacht was chartered by Ellen's lover, Lieutenant-Commander Miller, once of the Royal Navy, now trading under the name of Phoenix Island Fisheries at Canton Island. He intended to marry Ellen when his divorce was finalised. When he found he could not sell his fish at a good enough price, he headed for Samoa in April 1954, arriving in Apia, Western Samoa, in July. But his refrigeration had broken down and much of his cargo of fish had gone bad. He tried to sell it in Pago Pago but returned to Apia in March 1955, where he had to sell his whole cargo at rock-bottom prices.

He had to leave *Joyita* in Apia and returned to Canton Island. He was heavily in debt and some of his ship's papers were in the hands of the American authorities in Pago Pago where he had been unable to pay his harbour dues. Ellen Luomala told him to sell the yacht and settle his debts but he found that with his papers incomplete, no one wanted to buy it. It was in poor condition, with an unreliable radio and neglected engines.

The story of Miller's ill luck continued. He finally managed to get the yacht out of Apia and took on the job of transporting desperately needed food and medical supplies to the Fakaofo Islands, 200 miles way. As *Joyita* set sail from Apia on 2 October 1955, Samoans on the coast saw a mysterious, huge, dark vessel gliding in the *Joyita*'s wake. It seemed to make no noise but moved at considerable speed. It was certainly seen from *Joyita* because a message was radioed about its sighting.

On 10 November, a freighter found *Joyita* abandoned 90 miles north of Fiji, listing to port at 55 degrees. The radar gear was smashed and the logbook was missing. There was water in the hold but there was no hole. The radio was tuned in to a wavelength of 2182 kilocycles, the distress wavelength. The signal flags spelled out WNQV; no one ever has ever been able to interpret the signal and the fate of the crew of 25, including Miller, has never been discovered.

The yacht that was built by film director Roland West began its run of ill luck in 1931 – the breakdown of West's marriage, the death of Thelma Todd, the disasters that befell Miller – and ended in mystery in 1955. The fate of the *Joyita* has been attributed by many to a curse and its tale rates alongside that of the *Mary Celeste* as one of the sea's great unsolved mysteries.

Trouble on numerous films has been attributed to jinxes. When *The Exorcist* was being filmed at Burbank Studios in 1973 curious things happened. Props went missing, sets fell down, personnel were ill – people began to get the heebie-jeebies.

The film was based on the book by William Peter Blatty who based his story on a factual account of a 14-year-old boy who lived in a Washington suburb in 1949. The boy's parents had first noticed noises coming from his bedroom but could find no reason for them. The disturbances gradually became more violent and his bed shook. The family called in the Reverend

Winston who, although sceptical, spent the entire night of 18 February 1949 with the boy. By the morning, after witnessing furniture and objects moving around the room, the Reverend was convinced something extraordinary and unexplainable was going on and had the boy admitted to Georgetown Hospital. Tests revealed no mental or physical abnormalities and the disturbances did not stop.

The family finally called in a Roman Catholic priest to perform an exorcism. The priest performed the rites 30 times over a period of two months during which he witnessed the boy trembling violently and sometimes shouting in a voice that did not sound like his own. In May 1949, the final exorcism was performed and the disturbances ceased. The family were troubled no more.

For his book, Blatty chose to make the subject of the demonic possession a girl, played in the film by Linda Blair. Under the direction of William Friedkin, special effects wizards performed every trick they could muster to make the film the most spectacular horror film ever made. But those involved in it become increasingly anxious, believing that something sinister was going on. So William Friedkin, not taking any chances, asked for an exorcist to drive out the evil spirits holding up his production.

He was told that this was not a case for authentic exorcism and was refused an official rite. Not satisfied, he asked the film's technical adviser, Father Merrin, a Jesuit priest, to perform the exorcism. He did, since he was on the Warner Brothers' payroll.

William Peter Blatty was on set much of the time and later said, 'This one was scheduled for 105 days. It wound up being 200 days. We were plagued by strange and sinister things from the beginning.'

On its initial release, there were all sorts of stories about cold winds blowing through draught-free cinemas and of teenagers becoming so disturbed they became suicidal.

All this may seem fanciful showmanship and I would like to think it was. But it just so happened that when I joined the publicity department at Warner Brothers in London in 1973,

The Exorcist was the first film I had to work on. I went to see it at a midnight screening to which numerous celebrities had been invited as well as hundreds of other people from the media.

Now, this was not an audience unacquainted with the film industry and the make-believe world it creates. After half an hour I could not watch it any longer and, with chills running up and down my spine, I made my way out to the foyer. The place looked like a shelter of some kind as people sat about looking shaken and pale, men as well as women. I saw one man literally carried out of the auditorium, his legs completely turned to jelly.

This, to my knowledge, was not something that happened at every public showing thereafter; this was something unique. The reason I came out was because I really felt something was terribly wrong and could not bear to stay there any longer. I was frightened. And not because the film made me jump. There was just this pervading feeling of evil. And many others felt it. But not everyone. The vast majority of the audience remained in their seats and thoroughly enjoyed it. I recall Ryan O'Neal was there, virtually in the front row, loving it.

One of the Warner Brothers accounts girls, who watched it that night, suffered severe problems after that. She was too petrified to be left alone and had to sleep with her sister for months afterwards. When she took a shower this normally modest girl had to have the bathroom door left open. It may have been just an emotional response. But that is not the sort of response you normally expect a film to have on employees of the film company who made it.

I hated working on the film's publicity. My particular job was running the stills department. I could hardly bear to pick up the stills but, of course, I had to. Around that time, one of the offices was being painted. After lunch one day we returned to find that a tin of paint was lying on its side and the paint had poured out over the carpet. No one owned up to knocking the paint over. No one knew anything about it. It just appeared to happen.

Someone said, jokingly, 'It's *The Exorcist* curse!' At the time, I didn't doubt it. Today I have no rational explanation for my anxiety over that film. I have never seen it all the way through but that is not too surprising since it has never been on British TV and is not available on video in the UK. The reason for this is not completely clear, since the film was released on video for rental at the beginning of the video boom and then withdrawn when it was decided that every video had to be vetted by the censor.

Despite the film's enormous success, few associated with it seemed to have much luck following it. Director William Friedkin has not really been able to come up with another film to match its success and its young new star, Linda Blair, who was the possessed girl, really hit the skids when she was charged with possession of drugs. Ellen Burstyn, who played the girl's panic-stricken mum, peaked in her career in 1975 with *Alice Doesn't Live Here Any More* and despite her Oscar for that film, she never became a box-office star. Jason Miller, the young priest in the film, has been all but forgotten as an actor but enjoys success as a playwright. Lee J Cobb died shortly after the film and only Max Von Sydow, as the man of the title, seems to have survived to enjoy continuing success as a major character actor. But perhaps that is because he was such a wonderful Jesus in *The Greatest Story Ever Told...*

Lucifer struck the film industry again with *The Omen*, in which it was suggested that the Antichrist would come to this earth in the guise of a seemingly innocent boy who would grow to enjoy enormous financial power. Filming was bedevilled, or so some said. One stormy night, the film's screenwriter, David Seltzer, was aboard a passenger plane which was struck by lightning and apparently all passengers narrowly escaped death. On the same night, Gregory Peck, the star of the film, was also on board a plane that was struck by lightning.

While on location in London, director Richard Donner, was knocked down and seriously injured. John Richardson, the chief special effects director, was injured in another car accident while he was driving just outside a small Dutch town called, ominously, Ommen. The passenger in his car was killed. Richardson began to believe what many were whispering: that the film was jinxed.

During filming in a zoo, lions used in the scene went berserk and savaged two stuntmen and a keeper. The stuntmen survived but the keeper was killed.

Producer Harvey Bernhard always insisted the film was not jinxed and when I went on to the set of *The Omen 3: The Final Conflict* in 1979, he refused to discuss the subject. But when I had interviewed William Holden on the set of *Damien – Omen II* two years earlier, there was a different story. Holden, never the easiest man to interview, was sullen and dour and I only managed to get him talking at all because I showed an interest in his game ranch in Kenya. Films seemed to get in the way of his real interest – animal conservation – and he said he was only doing this one because, 'they paid me $750,000. That's a lot of money.'

But he was not happy making it. 'The script depresses me,' he said, 'and everything seems to be done for the purpose of sickening excess.'

So, I asked, what about the jinx that was supposed to hamper these films? He laughed and said, 'We began this damned film jinxed. Michael Hodges was going to direct it, then he was shown the back door and Don Taylor took over. Not that Don is a bad choice of director. But when the man at the helm gets replaced, it has to make you uneasy.'

Yes, I persisted, but is the film really jinxed? He replied philosophically, 'Is there a Devil? This film says there is. And if there is, maybe he doesn't like what we're saying. What's that old quote about there are more things in heaven and earth – and all that mystical stuff? How little we mere mortals understand. We like to dabble, not knowing what we're dabbling in. Look at Jayne Mansfield. She was supposed to be cursed – so they said – and she died in a most horrible way. It seems you can't do *Macbeth* without having disasters.'

Yes, I still persisted, but did he believe it?

'I don't disbelieve,' he said. He went on to say a whole lot more, but more of that later. As far as *The Omen* trilogy is concerned, it seems that bad luck really does in come in threes. As it happened, there was a fourth *Omen* but it was made for TV and really had nothing to do with the films Harvey Bernhard produced for the cinema.

The vogue for demonic films continued with the supposedly true story of *The Amityville Horror* and, again, incidents occurred that led to a belief that something sinister was interfering with its making. The film re-created the events experienced by the Lutz family after they moved into their dream house in the town of Amityville on Long Island in 1974. As a matter of course they called in a local priest to bless their $80,000 home and, during the ritual, the priest heard a male voice say, 'Get out.'

During the first two night in the house, the family heard strange noises at 3.15 am. On the third night George Lutz investigated the noises, again at 3.15 am, and found that the front door had been wrenched open and was hanging by a single hinge.

The incidents continued: windows opened and closed on their own and the staircase banister was ripped from the wall. One night George Lutz awoke to find his wife floating above the bed. When he pulled her down he found himself face to face with a hideous vision. Her appearance slowly returned to normal over the next six hours.

Now, if like me you would be disinclined to put up with any more of this, then you would wonder why the Lutzes did not move out there and then. They endured 28 days of horror before fleeing. It turned out that a young man had drugged his parents, brothers and sisters in that house and then shot each of them, at 3.15 am.

Author Jay Anson wrote the book after the Lutz family told him their story. The curse of the Amityville house had its effects on the author:

A woman to whom I loaned some early chapters took the manuscript home. She and two of her children were suffocated in a fire that night. The only item in the apartment that was not damaged by the fire was the manuscript. Another man put the manuscript in the trunk of his car and attempted to drive home. He drove through what he thought was a puddle. It turned out to be a 12-foot-deep hole into which his car slid. When the car was fished out the next day, the only dry object in it was the manuscript.

When my editor picked up the completed manuscript at my office his car caught fire and he discovered that all the bolts on his engine had been loosened.

A photographer was sent to take pictures of the house for the book's cover. Then he went to see Anson to take photographs of him. Outside Anson's house, the photographer's car caught fire. Soon after, Anson had a heart attack, and his son and a friend were almost killed in a car crash. The curse of the Amityville house had spread to everyone who was involved with it.

When the job of directing the film was offered to director Stuart Rosenberg he was hesitant but not because of the curse. He said, 'My first reaction was that it wouldn't be my cup of tea. But I read Jay Anson's book – and it had the ring of truth about it.' Perhaps wisely, it was decided that the film would not be shot in the actual house and an almost identical house in New Jersey was chosen. James Brolin, star of many films but perhaps best remembered for the glossy TV soap *Hotel*, played the part of George Lutz. He was certain the film was jinxed:

> On the first day of filming I stepped into the elevator in my apartment block and pressed the button for the lobby floor. Before we'd gone three floors it shuddered to a grinding, screeching halt, the lights flickered and I was plunged into frightening darkness. I screamed for help but nobody could hear me. It was an eerie, frightening experience. You imagine all sorts of hair-raising things in the silent darkness. My pleas bounced back like an echo. Those 30 minutes seemed an eternity.

On the second day of filming Brolin walked on the set, tripped over a cable and severely wrenched his ankle. He hobbled around for the next few days.

A curse was said to hang over anyone who tried to make a dramatic adaptation of Robert Graves's books, *I, Claudius* and *Claudius the God*. In 1937 Alexander Korda began producing the film of *I, Claudius*, starring Charles Laughton as Claudius and Merle Oberon as Messalina. Laughton looked to his director, Josef Von Sternberg, to help him find the character of Claudius. Instead, Von Sternberg treated Laughton with disdain, apparently feeling that Laughton needed to be shamed into getting to grips with the role.

Laughton came to feel he was a victim because he had once confessed to Von Sternberg that he was a homosexual; he felt he was now at his mercy. Filming became a torture for him. He forgot his lines, he began turning up late, then not turning up at all. He went wandering from one set to another, desperately trying to seek out Claudius.

Filming was delayed, costs mounted. Korda came under pressure from his financiers to get the film made. Then, as Merle Oberon was being driven to a wardrobe fitting, her studio car crashed and she was thrown through the windscreen. She was rushed to hospital where doctors feared they would discover internal injuries. Fortunately, she suffered little more than severe concussion and facial cuts. There were fears she would be scarred for life but as it turned out the surgeons saved her beautiful face.

However, as all these problems piled up on Korda's shoulders, he decided that shooting could not continue without Merle, who was going to be kept out of the picture for weeks. He abandoned production and it became known as *The Epic That Never Was*.

There were those of a superstitious nature who claimed that the whole project was jinxed, and that anyone who ever tried to make another film of *I, Claudius* would suffer a terrible fate. There were a couple of fruitless attempts though, one which should have starred Alec Guinness, but it just didn't get off the ground, despite the trend for big Roman epics like *Ben Hur*, *Quo Vadis* and *The Robe*. *I, Claudius* was considered to be bad luck for anyone who tried to dramatize it and no one dared to try again.

That is, until the BBC made their brilliant television series based on the two Robert Graves's books in 1977. An impressive cast of top British actors were lined up, including John Hurt who gave the definitive performance of Caligula. But the series was beset by problems, culminating in the death of producer Martin Lisemore in a car crash.

When I talked to John Hurt on the set of the supernatural thriller *The Shout*, the subject of the *I, Claudius* jinx came up. Not being one to suffer from superstition, I rather denigrated the idea that the series was jinxed.

Hurt said, 'There *is* a jinx. Martin Lisemore was killed in a car crash. It reminds me of when Merle Oberon, who was in the unfinished film, was injured in a car crash and stopped the picture being made.'

'Yes,' I said, 'but the series got made.'

'Yes, it *did* get made, but it *killed* the producer. Look, I'm not superstitious – intellectually I'm not – but you can't help but wonder when these things happen.'

And there's the rub. You can't help but wonder. Sometimes a curse or a jinx does not become a curse or a jinx until people begin to look back over a series of disasters and conclude that there is something unseen and unfathomable at work.

And that is what could well be happening at *Hello!* magazine. Its staple diet is photographic features on celebrities, concentrating on the positive aspects of their lives; the complete opposite of the *National Enquirer*, for instance, which focuses on the scandalous and the bizarre. But, they say (whoever *they* are) there is a curse on those who appear in *Hello!* and 'they' cite the following examples. Jane Seymour, star of many films including *Live and Let Die* and *Somewhere In Time*, and the TV series *Winds of War* and *Dr Quinn, Medicine Woman*, agreed to an article to celebrate her 40th birthday. In it she and husband David Flynn talked about their happy marriage. Before the article even appeared, their marriage had come to a sudden end.

Brigitte Bardot appeared, talking about her joy at being a wife, a mother and a grandmother. Shortly after she was rushed to

Crystal-Gazers

*During her reign in Hollywood between
1914 and 1919, Theda Bara (left) was
promoted as the first crystal-gazing star,
setting a trend that was to attract later
celebrities such as Rudolph Valentino and
Gloria Swanson, seen below resting
between scenes during the filming of*
Beyond the Rocks.

Ghosts

(Clockwise from top left) Blonde bombshell Kim Novak failed to endear herself to a pop music-hating ghost, while a mischievous spirit nearly burned down Elke Sommer's Hollywood home. The real Dick Turpin was still galloping about on Black Bess when TV's Turpin, Richard O'Sullivan, was filming the part in 1978, and Dame Anna Neagle saw Bath Theatre Royal's famous Grey Lady with her own eyes.

Near Death Experiences

It was during an emergency tracheotomy that Liz Taylor had a Near Death Experience. Peter Sellers (below left) saw himself being brought back to life after a major heart attack in 1964, while Michael Bentine found himself 'standing in the presence of eternity'.

Messages from Beyond

After Vivien Leigh died, she sent a message from 'the other side' saying that she still loved Laurence Olivier and was waiting for him (left). Peter Cushing, who was best remembered on screen for creating life from death (as below in Frankenstein Created Woman, *1967), looked forward to dying and becoming an artist 'the next time around'.*

Premonitions

While Sophia Loren's acute ESP has led to her describing herself as 'a witch' (above left), it was Bette Davis's mother whom Bette claimed had the stronger gift.

As a young actor, Cliff Robertson had a bizarre psychic experience involving a dream about his grandmother (below left). While Vincent Price learned of his friend Tyrone Power's death through a spectacular psychic message.

Superstitions

Actors have always been a superstitious breed: Tallulah Bankhead would have been mortified if her co-star Gary Cooper had entered her dressing room left foot first (above), while Douglas Fairbanks and Mary Pickford insisted on having their horoscopes presented to them daily (below left) and astrology ruled the life of Dr Who star Mary Tamm.

Curses

*While Jayne Mansfield believed there was a personal curse on her head (above left),
it was the car in which James Dean was killed that was said to be cursed (above right).
Both John Hurt (in* Caligula, *below left) and Trevor Howard (in* Mutiny on the
Bounty*) thought that the productions were jinxed.*

Curses

Margot Kidder and Christopher Reeve, seen above in Superman II, *were both victims of unrelated but horrendous accidents, while William Holden, seen below in* Damien: Omen II *with Lucas Donat (left) and Jonathan Scott-Taylor as the devilish son, said: 'we began this damned film jinxed'.*

Macbeth

'What hands are these?' asks Charlton Heston as Macbeth (left). But it was his nose that he should have worried about when it was nearly cut off in the fight scene. John Finch was the laird steeped in blood and Francesca Annis his Lady in Roman Polanski's ill-fated film of Macbeth (below).

Past Lives

Glenn Ford was at home on the range (as above in Cimarron*) possibly because he had been a real cowboy in a past life, while Diane Keene was a woman of Egypt, who saw her brother die under the wheels of an ancient cart.*

Close Encounters

An alien spaceship hovers over the Devil's Tower, but this time it's only a special effect from the UFO epic Close Encounters of the Third Kind, *during the shooting of which Steven Spielberg acquired the services of Dr J Allen Hynek, the man behind 'Project Blue Book'* (left).

Cult

When Tom Cruise fell for Nicole Kidman on the set of Days of Thunder, *he introduced her to the sci-fi cult of Scientology (above), of which Kirstie Alley and John Travolta are both members (below).*

hospital suffering from a drugs overdose. The gentry too have been struck by the *Hello!* curse. Viscount Althorp, brother of Princess Diana, presented his daughter Kitty in the pages of the magazine. Days later a scandal broke over his affair with cartoonist Sally Anne Lassoon. And less than a year before the Duke and Duchess of York split up, they had appeared in a colour spread to paint a portrait of a happy royal family.

In August 1994, Michael Jackson and Lisa Marie Presley gave *Hello!* the first exclusive pictures of the newly married couple. Apparently the couple were paid a huge fee, as are all the celebrities who pose so happily for the *Hello!* photographers. At the time of writing, the couple have not been seen publicly for a considerable time and rumours that they have split up are flying thick and fast. Time will tell, of course.

It should not be forgotten that there are scores of others who have appeared in the magazine who have not suffered terrible fates and the so-called *Hello!* curse remains more a tabloid invention than an authentic jinx.

When things keep going wrong you can't help but wonder... That's why, when I was at *Photoplay*, I wrote an open letter to director David Lean who was deep in preparations to make his version of the story of the mutiny on the *Bounty.*

At the time I wrote it, in 1980, it seemed little more than an editorial bit of nonsense, inspired by the recollection I had that the 1962 version of *Mutiny on the Bounty*, with Marlon Brando and Trevor Howard, was supposedly jinxed; a notion rienforced by the fact that on the day I was to be taken to see the film by my parents, I fell down the stairs at school and broke my ankle. Unable to go to see it – to my great distress – someone told me then that the film had a jinx on it. My young mind wondered if I had fallen victim to the *Bounty* jinx. It's hardly likely.

Years later the idea of a *Bounty* jinx gave me the idea of the open letter to David Lean (who probably never read it anyway) and I began looking into the background to the previous films. It did start me wondering if there was something behind the so-called jinx.

The first major version (ignoring the forgotten amateurish Australian production *In the Wake of the Bounty* with an unknown Errol Flynn in 1933) was made by MGM in 1935 with Charles Laughton as Captain Bligh and Clark Gable as Fletcher Christian. That film showed Bligh to be a monster, a merciless man who drove his sailors beyond all human endurance. It has since been disputed that Bligh was ever a monster and that Christian was not the hero he had always been portrayed as.

Filming was stormy to say the least. Clark Gable did not want to make the film. He hated the idea of having to play an Englishman and refused to even attempt to lose his American accent. But MGM, who had him tied to a watertight contract, gave him no choice in the matter. They also told him he had to shave off his famous moustache. That was too much for him. He refused and threatened to walk out and never come back but, in the end, he had to shave off his moustache and get on with the miserable experience.

He and a number of the film crew were almost killed when a water taxi transporting them crashed into a rock. Most of the passengers, including the driver, were drunk after an all-night binge. Their yells alerted a nearby boat and luckily all hands were saved.

The film's director, Frank Lloyd, and the associate producer, Al Lewin, quarrelled constantly. Finally, Lloyd told Irving Thalberg, the boy wonder of MGM, 'This picture isn't big enough for the two of us and you have to choose between me and Lewin.'

Thalberg responded, 'I'm sorry to hear that, Frank. It'll hurt me to fire you.' Lloyd went back to work on the picture without another complaint to Thalberg but the verbal battles continued.

Laughton was miserable throughout filming. He was desperate to prevent any hint of his homosexuality to show on screen. Opposite the manly Clark Gable, Laughton was plagued with doubts and fear that he would appear to walk in a mincing way or gesture effeminately.

The result on screen was a triumph, despite all the gremlins, and the huge box office takings inspired MGM to remake it in

1962. They sent producer Aaron Rosenberg to Marlon Brando who agreed to do the film provided he could have a certain amount of artistic control. Rosenberg wanted him to play Bligh; he wanted to play Christian. Rosenberg agreed.

Carol Reed was assigned to direct. Eric Ambler's screenplay went through various rewrites by some of Hollywood's finest talent, including Billy Wilder. Even Brando wrote his own version which Rosenberg rejected. Credit for the screenplay was finally given to Charles Lederer.

The weather in Tahiti, where the film was mainly shot, was appalling, and production was constantly being held up. Then Carol Reed resigned. He and Rosenberg could not agree over their concepts of Bligh, played this time by Trevor Howard. Reed had also clashed with Brando. He had had enough and left Tahiti, while Rosenberg brought in Lewis Milestone to direct.

Said Milestone of his first weeks on Tahiti, 'I knew Brando and I were going to have a stormy passage right from the start. Brando likes to discuss every scene for hours. I felt time was being wasted. The next thing I knew, Rosenberg was on the set every day and Brando was arguing with him instead of me. It was a terrible way to make a picture.'

A number of hell-raising actors got into trouble: Trevor Howard got into a drunken fight and spent a night in a police cell. Richard Harris raised plenty of hell in local taverns and ended up refusing to act alongside Marlon Brando. Welsh actor Hugh Griffith caused so much trouble due to the demon drink that he was thrown off the island. His character disappeared completely from the film.

Milestone endured four months of filming on Tahiti and, by the end of it, was hardly directing the film at all. He said that Brando gave instructions to the cameraman and all Milestone did was put his feet up and shout 'Action!' When the unit returned to Hollywood to film Brando's death scene, Milestone refused to have anything to do with it, so another director was brought in to make the scene to Brando's specifications.

The film had begun with an estimated $8 million budget, an impressive amount then. By the time the film was in the can, it had cost 19 million. The film grossed just 13 million.

All of these stories served me well in writing my open letter to Lean. The article was headed, 'Dear David, Beware of the '*Bounty* Jinx!' When I mentioned this to Trevor Howard, he said, 'Don't just write an article. Get on the bloody phone and tell him. There probably is a jinx. And it's probably Captain Bligh, thoroughly fed up with the way he's been painted as the biggest villain to sail the highs seas.'

By this time, Lean, who had not made a film since *Ryan's Daughter* in 1970, had spent more than a year in the south Pacific working on the screenplay with Robert Bolt. His idea was to make two films, the first leading up to the mutiny, the second about the fate of the mutineers. All the major studios read the scripts. All the major studios turned them down, estimating each of the two films would cost in the region of $25 million.

As the stress of the project increased and it began to look like it would never get off the ground, Robert Bolt suffered a stroke and a heart attack. Lean retired to his Switzerland retreat. Then, out of the blue, his old friend Sam Spiegel, who produced Lean's *Bridge on the River Kwai* and *Lawrence of Arabia*, turned up to persuade him to rework his two screenplays into one. It all seemed ready to proceed again, and Anthony Hopkins was approached to play Captain Bligh. This time Bligh would not be portrayed as a ruthless tyrant. That was the situation at the time of my open letter.

After that Lean dropped out, and so did Spiegel. Italian producer Dino De Laurentiis stepped in to produce, Orion Pictures in Hollywood took it on, and New Zealand director Roger Donaldson was hired to direct the film. Hopkins still wanted to play Bligh and Christopher Reeve was cast as Fletcher Christian. But Robert Bolt's script was altered to the point that Reeve, furious over the changes, pulled out six weeks before it was scheduled to begin filming on the island of Moorea, near Tahiti.

Australian actor Mel Gibson, then known to American audiences only as *Mad Max*, took on the role. At that time he was hitting the bottle hard, and he managed to get into a fight at the

Tattoo night club in which a Coke bottle over his head put him in hospital. The filming schedule was rearranged to allow for his cuts and bruises being patched up. He seemed to be yet another *Mutiny on the Bounty* hellraiser, following in the wake of Hugh Griffith, Richard Harris and Trevor Howard. And he found little sympathy from Hopkins, a recently reformed alcoholic who was concentrating on keeping himself on the wagon.

It has been said that Gibson was drinking heavily to help him forget that the film was already feeling like an unmitigated disaster. His estimation was based on the daily rushes which somehow did not live up to the $20 milion budget being lavished on the production.

Hopkins had his own problems. He found himself in contention with the director and they engaged in some epic rows on the set, sometimes in front of hundreds of extras. Hopkins had immersed himself so totally in the role that some felt that he was behaving on the set as Bligh might have done. But Hopkins was unhappy with Donaldson's approach to film making and the final straw almost came when Donaldson rewrote some of Robert Bolt's screenplay. Hopkins stormed off and had to be persuaded to come back.

Hopkins, on reflection, admits he did not behave totally admirably but he insists he always had the film's best interests at heart. He was also still something of a newcomer to films and had to learn to deal with the collaborative methods of film making.

Filming continued uneasily and, ultimately, the results were disappointing. The new *Mutiny on the Bounty* ran for seven weeks in America where it took around $6 million dollars. The final cost of the film was estimated at $40 million.

In retrospect it is not difficult to conclude that *Mutiny on the Bounty* was jinxed, but it *is* difficult to discover a reason. At least with the Devil films, you could presume that satanic forces might have been involved but what makes a film project like *Mutiny on the Bounty* jinxed? Perhaps it has something to do with the fact that the real voyage was, in essence, born out of an evil, the evil of slavery. The *Bounty*'s mission was to bring back breadfruit trees from Tahiti as food for the slaves in the West Indies. The food was cheap and energizing – ideal to maintain slaves. But the bread-fruits were never given to the slaves. The mutiny aboard the *Bounty* brought the whole project to an abrupt end.

As for the crew of the *Bounty*, there appeared to be no clear winners. The fate of the mutineers remains uncertain and Captain Bligh, who was apparently a brilliant seaman and not the villain literature and films have portrayed him to be, was literally *blighted* by the incident. So maybe Trevor Howard had a point when he intimated that the ghost of Bligh was behind all the troubles.

It is in retrospect also that they are now saying that *Superman* is jinxed. Bad luck seems to have dogged the super-hero, or at least many who have been associated with the film. It began with the acquisition of the super-hero by Marvel Comics from creators Jerry Siegel and Joe Shuster, who were paid a meagre amount for the copyright. Perhaps Siegel and Shuster were just so over the moon to be paid something for their comic-strip creation that they did not stop to consider that *Superman* might become a million-dollar enterprise. So, Siegel and Shuster were definitely not the lucky ones.

Screen *Superman* number one was Kirk Alyn who starred in the Columbia serial in 1948. He never was a particularly good actor, coming from a vaudeville background before getting some minor roles in minor films. In 1946 he became a star in *Daughter of Don Q*, a movie serial, then a popular form of cinema entertainment. Serials were cheap to make, quick to film and kept a lot of people employed. The first *Superman* serial came in 1948, and suddenly Alyn was a star of sorts. Two years later he was back in tights and cape for *Atom Man vs Superman*. He tried to break away from the part by refusing to make any more *Superman* serials. Apart from a couple of more forgettable films, he was unable to shake off the role and, without other work, he wrote his memoirs, *A Job for Superman*, which he had to publish himself. In 1977 he sued a comics publishing company and two film companies for $10 million for using his picture on a plaque which showed him on a window ledge in his Superman outfit, with the words 'Super Schmuck'. At the time of writing, he lives in Arizona, a victim of Alzheimer's disease.

Screen *Superman* number two was George Reeves who starred in the TV series of the 1950s. Previously he had enjoyed a brisk and busy career playing minor roles in good and bad films, including *Gone With the Wind*, *Samson and Delilah* and *From Here to Eternity*. *Superman* made him a household name, even in Japan where Emperor Hirohito wrote to tell him how much he enjoyed the show.

But once he was a TV star, the film business turned its back on him. No one, reasoned the studios, could see him as anything else but Superman. Reeves was despondent and, so the story goes, on 6 June 1959, he shot himself in the head with a 9 mm Luger at his Benedict Canyon home at around one o'clock in the morning.

There are some curious aspects to his death and it has been suggested he was murdered by the former general manager of MGM, Eddie Mannix, for messing about with his wife, Toni. Two months before his death, Reeves complained to the Los Angeles District Attorney that he was being plagued with anonymous phone calls. He was convinced Toni Mannix was the caller. But his fiancée, Lenore Lemmon, blamed Superman for his death, saying that the role had so dominated his life and he had become so identified with the role, that it became impossible for him to get other parts.

For some curious reason Lenore had been downstairs at the time of Reeves's death. Some friends rang the doorbell, and Lemmon, who was already up, let them in. Reeves, irritated at being disturbed, came downstairs, threatening to throw them out.

He went back upstairs and Lemmon said, 'Now he's opening the drawer to get the gun.' There was a gun shot. She said, 'See, I told you; he's shot himself.'

Reeves left the majority of his estate to Toni Mannix.

Superman number three was Christopher Reeve. Perhaps his very name, Reeve, was not a good omen, although when he was plucked from obscurity to star in the blockbuster *Superman – The Movie* in 1977, the publicity machine was quick to point out that his surname was merely a lucky coincidence. Filming began in Rome, but had to be abandoned when it proved too big a project for the Italian studios.

Production moved between England, Canada and America. Shooting in New York coincided with the infamous 1977 blackout. Director Richard Donner had the cast and crew all ready to roll in temperatures of 104 degrees when the power went off. Tempers were frayed to say the least.

The screenplay originally included a scene featuring Lois Lane's parents. Noel Neill, who played Lois in the TV series, was cast as Lois's mother. Filming the scene in Calgary, Canada, was interrupted by a tremendous thunderstorm which uprooted trees and turned the location into something of a disaster area. The scene was abandoned.

Superman II was to be filmed simultaneously with Part One as the producers had already decided there would be a sequel. But it proved not to be quite that simple. Sarah Douglas, who played Ursa, told me, 'Parts One and Two should have been shot together. They concentrated on Part Two to begin with and we hardly did anything on Part One. I did nine months' work first time round and obviously it didn't take all that time just for the three-minute sequence I was in at the beginning of Part One. So they shelved Part Two to be completed the following year.'

By the time the cast and crew were reassembled for the bulk of shooting *Superman II*, the producers had fired their original director Richard Donner and replaced him with Richard Lester. The cast was split into two camps – those for and those against the move. Margot Kidder, who played Lois Lane, was outraged, saying that Donner was the man who made the first film the success it later became.

Sarah Douglas did not like the idea of firing the man who had seen them through thick and thin but, she told me, 'Richard Donner took endless days to shoot scenes. With Richard Lester if you didn't get it right on the second take you were in a lot of trouble. I did enjoy working more with Lester and had much more fun with Part Two.'

Apart from the near mutiny, there were other problems on Part Two. 'They discovered they hadn't shot the destruction of Metropolis with Part One,' said Sarah Douglas, 'and they were by no means ready to do it. They hadn't worked out how the hell to do it. In the two years' duration between Parts One and Two they had concentrated on perfecting a way of flying and by the time we came back Richard Donner had gone and we had to start again.' She also said there were further problems among the cast:

> It was English vs Americans in the end. Margot was on her second divorce by the time we got into Part Two, having gone through her first divorce on Part One, so that was all a bit trying. Christopher – what can I say? I think he was getting a bit wrapped up in Superman. We all started work on the first day together, and by the end of the film Chris couldn't remember any of our names. But having said that, I admit that you do almost get taken over by these characters and it's very difficult to cut off from that. But I was a little disappointed to find he didn't remember who I was or my name.

Tragedies struck cast and crew of the first film and its three sequels. During the filming of *Superman IV* in 1986, stunt man John Lees suffered terrible injuries to his legs when a wire hoisting him up at Elstree Studios snapped, sending him crashing 20 feet. He had been earning £50,000 a year but suddenly his career was over. He successfully sued Cannon Films who were found to be negligent.

In November 1990, Margot Kidder was filming a TV show in Canada when she was flung from the open-top car she was driving. It happened when the newly installed power brakes in the 1961 convertible proved so powerful that when Kidder put her foot on the brake pedal, the car stopped violently, her seat flew forward, and she was flung out of the car.

She suffered nerve damage, some paralysis and painful spasms in her limbs. She spent months in a wheelchair, at first unsure she would ever walk again. Happily, she has since recovered.

Just a few months later, in March 1991, Lee Quigley, who had played the baby Superman at the age of seven months in the first film, died after sniffing an aerosol. He was 14.

Then tragedy struck Christopher Reeve himself in May 1995. A keen horseman, he was at a show-jumping event in Virginia, where he keeps a stable of hunters and show-jumpers, when his horse reared up and he fell. Helmut Bohen, who was assisting at the ground, said, 'When I reached him he was unconscious and was not breathing. I gave him mouth-to-mouth. All the blood drained from his face. At first it seemed as if he wouldn't make it. The medics started banging on his chest, then he began breathing again.'

Reeve was flown to the University of Virginia's Medical Center in Charlottesville. They found he had a blood clot on his brain and a fracture in a crucial part of the neck vertebrae, paralysing him from the neck down. Unable to breathe unassisted, he was put on a life-support machine. The blood clot was inoperable in the short term and doctors feared that it could move and kill him.

Pneumonia set in and, as doctors finally prepared to operate to insert metal rods into his neck, they gave him a five to ten per cent chance of survival. The operation was a success and, little more than a month later, Reeve was in an electric wheelchair. But he remains paralysed and unable to breathe without a respirator.

On American television, in an interview with Barbara Walters, he said that he had considered, 'for ten minutes', telling the doctors to turn off his life support. But when he saw his wife and children, and all who loved him, he realized he was really 'a lucky man'.

I have interviewed Reeve a number of times since I first met him in 1978 when he was promoting the first *Superman* film. I have always found him immensely likeable. It may be that he did let success go to his head for a while, but he did come down to earth to establish himself as one of the nicest of Hollywood stars. If he ever walks again, it will be a miracle.

Now, some may say that miracles do happen. And not always

to those who are of a religious persuasion. In direct opposition to those films and people who appear to have suffered from some jinx or curse, whether real or imaginary, here is a story about a film which, its director said, was only completed because of 'a miracle'.

In 1966 John Frankenheimer made the classic MGM-Cinerama racing film, *Grand Prix*. As well as actors like James Garner, Yves Montand and Toshiro Mifune, the film also featured 32 professional racing car drivers. In 1980 when I interviewed Frankenheimer, just mentioning the film brought him out in a cold sweat. I asked him if it had been a dangerous film to make. He said, 'It was a miracle that not one of those drivers was killed that year.' For once, here was a case of a film blessed and there was no doubt in Frankenheimer's mind that the picture was completed because of a miracle or two:

> If just one driver had been killed, that would have been the end of the film. The following year six of them were killed. One of them was Lorenzo Bandini who was killed at Monte Carlo right at the same spot he had helped me to stage an accident. That was for the scene in which James Garner's car went into the water. We used the Monte Carlo rescue team for that. I told them we were going to throw James Garner into the water and I said, 'You guys get him out as fast as you can.'
> 'We are ze best in ze world,' they told me.
> I went to Garner and said, 'How do you feel about it?'
> 'It's colder than hell in that water,' he replied.
> 'But do you want to do it?'
> He said, 'Sure, but do you really think they'll get me out?'
> I said, 'Absolutely. They'll get you out for sure.'
> So in went Garner. I said, 'Roll the cameras,' and told the rescue team, 'right, in you go.'
> Now those cameras hold eight minutes of film. We ran out of film before they even got to him. Garner almost *drowned*, and then they almost ran over him with the rescue boat.

One year later Bandini crashed at the same spot but he didn't go into the water. By the time the rescue team got to him his car was in flames and he burned to death. They *should* have got him out, but nothing worked. The fire extinguishers weren't loaded. If that had happened during filming on the first race, the film would have been over.

Of course, I didn't tell Metro-Goldwyn-Mayer that. How they ever let the film be made, I'll never know. Out of the 32 drivers I used, 21 are now dead. The fact that nobody got hurt on that movie is a miracle.

If something can be cursed, then it is logical to assume it can be blessed. And at this point of writing, I cannot help but think that miracles do happen. I really hope so. Especially for Christopher Reeve.

8

The Curse of *Macbeth*

Everyone involved in theatre knows that there are certain things you *never* do. Such as whistle in the wings. To do so will summon disaster. There is actually some foundation to this otherwise irrational superstition. In days long gone, stagehands used to raise and lower scenery in response to whistled signals from the stage manager. An innocent whistle from the wrong person at the wrong time could result in havoc. So today whistling in the wings, or even in the dressing rooms, is enough to turn some actors into nervous wrecks. But to push an actor to the verge of a nervous breakdown, one has only to utter the dreaded title of that Shakespearean Scottish play – *Macbeth*.

It is common among actors, directors, producers and technicians, whether on a film or in a theatre, or anywhere they happen to be, never ever to mention *Macbeth*. It has to be referred to as 'The Scottish Play'. Just being in the play is considered an ill omen and bad luck will befall you. In my case, it was a heavy broadsword that befell – right on my nose. I was in the middle of the sword fight, telling Macduff, 'Thou losest labour,' when he did lose labour and his sword which, at that moment, he was holding above his head as I grappled with him. His sword, a really heavy broadsword – not plastic – cut my nose, making the sword fight sequence remarkably realistic as warm blood trickled down my face as I carried on regardless, wondering if my nose was broken. Fortunately it wasn't. But the audience watched in horror, wondering if this was some incredibly clever special effect or a real-life out-take.

So why did I nearly have my nose sliced off during my fight with Macduff? And why does ill-luck plague the play, whether performed on stage or on film? Well, it seems that the famous 'Double, double, toil and trouble' witches' incantation is responsible. Some scholars claim it was taken from a book of contemporary witches' spells so it may be an actual spell. It has to be remembered that in Shakespeare's time, witches were regarded as a real phenomenon. It is certainly an interesting theory that whenever the play is performed, the three witches manage to cast a spell over each and every performance. Or maybe the curse was set in motion the very first time it was said, and nothing can save it. As Anton La Vey told Jayne Mansfield, a curse cannot be revoked.

The play's royal première at Hampton Court before James I, around 1605, was a disaster. The young king was so outraged by it that he had it banned. It seems that being the son of Mary, Queen of Scots who was beheaded at the command of Elizabeth I, he was squeamish about assassination, witchcraft and madness – the three basic themes of the play. So *Macbeth*'s première was the first and last reported performance for five years.

It reappeared at the Globe Theatre in London in 1610. Three years later the Globe burned down, and all the props, sets and costumes for *Macbeth* were destroyed. Shakespeare died three years after that and, when some superstitious souls came to the conclusion that the play itself was under a curse, no one dared to stage it again for about fifty years.

It was being performed at London's Covent Garden in 1703 when one of the worst storms in history struck the country. Hundreds of seamen were lost in the hurricane and much of the capital was damaged. Bristol was all but destroyed. It was declared by God-and-witch-fearing moralists that *Macbeth* had angered God. He had displayed His displeasure at the evil promoted in the play by sending the torrential rain and wind.

Some theatres continued to brave the curse by staging the play and, in 1731, it was put on at London's Portugal Street Theatre where an argument among members of the audience turned into a riot. A fire was started and the place nearly burned down. Covent Garden dared to open its 1808 autumn season with the play. Before a month was out the theatre had burned to the ground and 23 people were killed.

In 1849, New York's Astor Place Opera House featured

English actor William Charles Macready and American actor Edwin Forrest in the play. Unfortunately, the two actors hated each other and the play was troubled by their feud which reached a climax during the last performance when a mob of Forrest's fans stoned the theatre and smashed windows. The militia were summoned and a full-scale riot ensued. The militia fired upon the crowd and about 20 people fell dead. Scores more were injured.

In 1937 Laurence Olivier had the title role at the Old Vic in a production fraught with the now familiar problems. Michael St Denis, the director, and actress Vera Lindsey were injured in a taxi-cab accident. Then Olivier caught a cold and lost his voice, delaying the opening for four days, which as it turned out, was a blessing in disguise since the play was not ready for the original opening night.

As rehearsals continued, Lillian Baylis, manager of the Old Vic, fell ill but sent a message to the director that her illness should not hold up the opening any further. She also sent a message to Olivier: 'May you be as happy in *Macbeth* as in *Hamlet* last season.'

She had a fatal heart attack before the opening night. The cast and crew were shattered. But, of course, they had to go on, as the show always does. During one of the preview nights, Olivier's sword blade broke during the fight scene between Macbeth and Macduff. The broken blade flew into the audience and hit a gentleman who died of a heart attack.

One evening a stage weight fell, just missing Olivier. Had it hit him, he would have undoubtedly been killed. Not too surprisingly, he hated the whole wretched experience. In particular, he blamed himself and his director for the play's artistic failings which had brought a hail of criticism from the press. 'We arty lot were going through a phase of avid preoccupation with size; everything had to suggest godlike proportions,' he said. In keeping with this philosophy of 'godlike proportions', the cast wore mask-like make up which was so big that Vivien Leigh was prompted to note, 'You hear Macbeth's first line, then Larry's make-up comes on, then Banquo comes on, then Larry comes on!'

Olivier recalled, 'Noël Coward nearly died laughing when he came to see it.' Despite all this it was a huge financial success, as the play invariably is because, despite the curse, it remains popular with audiences. It is just a disaster for those performing and producing it. It was then transferred for an extended run to the New Theatre. 'A strange thing' was how Olivier summed up his surprise at its success.

In 1947 the play was produced in Oldham, where Harold Norman played the title role. He broke the golden rule that forbids anyone to recite the play anywhere but on stage as he rehearsed in his dressing room. During the final scene, in which Macduff kills Macbeth, Norman was accidentally stabbed. It was only a slight wound but an infection set in and he died a month later.

Charlton Heston has played Macbeth a number of times on stage and, while he acknowledges that a traditional curse hangs over the play, he never shies away from doing it. He loves the play and has triumphed in it more than once on the American stage. But even the man who played Michelangelo and Biblical figures like Moses and John the Baptist found he was not immune from the curse.

His first professional Macbeth was an open-air production in Bermuda in 1952 under the direction of Burgess Meredith. Said Heston, 'I remember when I was run over by a motorcycle the afternoon of opening in Bermuda.' He picked himself up, brushed himself off, and bruised and sore, went on to do the show.

The death of Lady Macbeth was turned into a farce during one performance. Meredith had decided to have a dummy representing her as she throws herself from the ramparts to her death. Just as the dummy was hurled from the stage, a strong gust of wind blew it back on. The actor playing the messenger gravely announced to Heston, 'The Queen is dead, my Lord,' and the audience roared with laughter.

Heston was the Scots laird once again in 1975, performing at the Ahmanson Theatre in Los Angeles. Vanessa Redgrave was his Lady Macbeth and Richard Jordan was Macduff. During an afternoon rehearsal Jordan tripped over a cable and sprained his ankle.

'After much debate, the listed understudy went on in the part for the preview audience, reading much of it,' said Heston. 'Of course he didn't know the combat scene and couldn't possibly do it. Tony de Longis, who'd helped Joe Canutt stage the combats and played Young Siward, got up after I'd killed him, and (as Macduff) killed me, carrying through the rest of the scene. It worked well enough, and the audience, as they usually do in emergencies, rose to the occasion.'

Then Vanessa Redgrave came down with flu and had to stand down for her understudy to take over for a while. Four nights before the play closed, Heston came close to losing his famous beaked nose.

Into the last phase of the combat with Macduff, my sword blade snapped at the hilt, probably from metal fatigue. I was holding a head parry at the time. How Jordan's blade didn't slice my face open, I don't know. Perhaps he pulled his stroke, perhaps I was quick enough to duck back a bit. It only nicked the mended bone in my nose. [There was] very little blood, but it scared the hell out of me. I lay dead under the stairs through Richard's last speech, panting and wet with sweat, tasting the blood on my face in the dark, trying to tell which was real and which was prop.

Before he became famous in films, Orson Welles directed a bizarre version of *Macbeth* at the Lafayette Theatre in Harlem. He and producer John Houseman set it in Haiti to give it an authentic voodoo background and cast genuine Haitian voodooists to play the parts intended for the witches. Only one critic slated the production, Percy Hammond of the *Herald Tribune*. The outraged voodooists staged an all-night session of cursing in the theatre, complete with chanting and drumming.

The next day Hammond fell ill with a chill. Within days it developed into pneumonia and he died.

Welles had long wanted to make a film version of *Macbeth*. Despite his initial triumph with *Citizen Kane* only seven years before, Hollywood had quickly become disenchanted with him as his subsequent films failed to attract audiences and no one wanted to touch his version of *Macbeth*. But determined to go ahead, Welles went to Republic, the studio which specialized in low-budget westerns and action films. Their only major pictures starred John Wayne. Obviously, Republic did not quite see John Wayne in the role of *Macbeth*.

However, Herbert Yates, the studio head, listened intently as Welles pitched *Macbeth* at him. The whole idea of a prestige movie at the studio appealed to Yates but he told Welles they had limited finances. Welles assured him it could be shot in 21 days.

So, in 1948, with Yates's blessing, Welles went ahead producing, directing and starring in the film that became the biggest disaster in the small studio's history. He brought the film in on time but it was a shambles. He had his actors inflect a sort of Scots dialect, which nobody could understand, not even in Scotland. The sets looked like cardboard, and much of the supporting cast, who had no classical training, were appalling.

The film was greeted with dreadful reviews and hardly any interest from the public. Welles left Hollywood to embark on a career in Europe. The film is now looked upon by some as a minor masterpiece – but only by a dedicated few.

In 1967 Peter Hall directed Paul Schofield in a new stage version for the Royal Shakespeare Company. It was another ill-fated production and proved a personal disaster for Hall who suffered from shingles and depression throughout rehearsals. Hall returned to the play in 1978, directing Albert Finney in the role at the National Theatre. It was another unhappy experience for Hall, who had embarked on the production reluctantly, having promised Finney he would do it. There were many times when he must have wished he could renege on his promise.

*

In 1971 Roman Polanski directed a striking film version of *Macbeth*. He threw himself into it on the heels of the death of his wife Sharon Tate at the hands of the murdering disciples of Charles Manson.

Polanski had begun his career in Poland as an actor and then turned his hand to directing films. He worked in France for a while, making something of a fine reputation for himself, before arriving in the UK to make his classics *Repulsion* and *Cul-de-Sac*. Hollywood inevitably beckoned and he shot to prominence in 1968 with the devil film *Rosemary's Baby*.

There was a long break after that, due mainly to his wife's murder in August 1969. Perhaps ominously, he chose *Macbeth* as his return to film making. But then, bad luck had plagued Polanski most of his life, which had begun in the Jewish ghettos of Cracow during the Nazi occupation. Most of his family, including his mother, died in concentration camps. He spent his war years just managing to avoid being caught by the Nazis.

Polish film producer, Andrzej Munk, who gave him his first job, died in a car crash. David Stone, who translated Polanski's French screenplay of *Repulsion* into English, died of appendicitis. Composer Krzysztof Komeda, who wrote the music for Polanski's films up to *Rosemary's Baby*, died jumping from a train. Françoise Dorleac, who starred in *Cul-de-Sac*, died in a car crash. Then came the tragedy with Sharon Tate. The filming of *Macbeth* began with a bad omen. Polanski had chosen to show every gory aspect of all the murders and deaths which, when performed in the theatre, usually occur off-stage. For the scene in which Lady Macduff's children are murdered, he wanted to cover a four-year-old girl in fake blood and he began to explain to the child how she must lie down and pretend to be dead. While he applied the fake blood to her face, he asked her her name.

'Sharon,' she replied. Polanksi turned pale.

There were endless difficulties throughout filming in Wales as Polanski, producing for the first time without his usual partner, Gene Gutowski, fought with the actors, the crew and the film's backers. Kenneth Tynan, who worked on the screenplay with

Polanski, felt that the director was 'steeling himself' against his sorrow over Sharon's murder.

Often during the filming of *Macbeth*, Polanski admitted that it was not worth continuing to make films. 'Yes, I have those moments,' he said. 'When I was making *Macbeth* and Sharon had been killed, and it was a very unhappy period.'

The film was a critical and commercial failure – but a fine film none the less, I hasten to add – and Polanski did not return to Hollywood for two years, going back in 1973 to make *Chinatown*, which was a huge success. But after that his films were forgettable. Then, in 1977, he pleaded guilty to a charge of statutory rape, and fled to France to escape imprisonment.

When *Empire* asked him in 1992 if he felt like a man who had been cursed, he replied, 'Oh, yes.' The combination of the classic *Macbeth* curse and the Polanski curse could not have boded well for anyone involved in the 1971 film version.

The British actor John Finch was excellent in the title role of Polanski's *Macbeth*. He had made several films previously and was all set to become a major star. He was dashing, handsome and a fine actor. After *Macbeth* he starred in Robert Bolt's disappointing *Lady Caroline Lamb* and Hitchcock's appalling *Frenzy*. Then Finch became ill and diabetes was diagnosed. He all but disappeared from the film scene for several years. When he did return, he had missed the boat to film stardom.

Lady Macbeth was played by Francesca Annis who, prior to *Macbeth*, had enjoyed a varied and promising film career with pictures like *Cleopatra*, *Murder Most Foul* and *The Walking Stick*. After *Macbeth*, her film career also faltered, although she has enjoyed success on the stage and TV. But film stardom, which she deserved, was not to be.

In 1980 came perhaps the most infamous stage version of *Macbeth* ever when Peter O'Toole played the laird who would be king at the Old Vic. Bryan Forbes, director of such films as *Whistle Down the Wind* and *King Rat*, took the helm of this version when the original director, Jack Gold, dropped out – 'possibly after consulting his astrologer,' Forbes noted in retrospect.

In his book, *A Divided Life*, Bryan Forbes wrote, 'I was well aware of the curse of *Macbeth*; the superstition is burnt into every actor's soul from an early age.' Yet he accepted the task of helping O'Toole make his return to the stage after an absence of 17 years during which he had become a major film star in *Lawrence of Arabia, Lord Jim* and a host of far more forgettable films. Not surprisingly, by the time he came to do *Macbeth*, he felt that his career had become 'tepid'. He had also undergone surgery and, as a consequence, given up the demon drink which had been a staple part of his diet for years.

He was determined to prove himself and had joined the Old Vic company which was in collaboration with Timothy West's Prospect Theatre Company. O'Toole and West were joint artistic directors but, according to Forbes, the two men did not enjoy a happy working relationship. O'Toole maintained complete artistic control and let West balance the books. West would have liked to have had a creative hand but O'Toole kept him at arm's length.

Rehearsals were generally uneventful but, as opening night approached, O'Toole suddenly decided he hated the set design and fired the man responsible. Forbes had to find a replacement at short notice. Then O'Toole rejected the costumes designed especially for the production and Forbes had to find another replacement.

Forbes had no problem working with O'Toole but was alarmed from time to time by the actor's flamboyant and somewhat dangerous manner. O'Toole kept reminding Forbes that the play was 'steeped in blood'. He asked the director, 'Do you know how many times the word blood appears in the text?' Forbes didn't, so O'Toole told him. Later, O'Toole informed Forbes that if you stab a living man, the blood spurts 17 feet. Forbes urged O'Toole not to get carried away with the bloody aspect of the play. His words fell on deaf ears.

When Princess Margaret visited the theatre during rehearsals, O'Toole began telling her about the play being 'steeped in blood'. She told him, 'What you need is some Kensington Gore. We use it all the time in St John Ambulance demonstrations. It's very realistic.'

So O'Toole sent an assistant stage manager to buy several gallons of Kensington Gore which was poured into a zinc bath in his quick-change room.

On the opening night, Forbes discovered O'Toole in his dressing room virtually naked. 'Aren't you leaving it a bit late to get into costume?' the director inquired.

'Can't wear them, darling,' O'Toole replied. 'They're hopeless.'

Panic-stricken that O'Toole had lost his nerve, Forbes sought out Brian Blessed who was playing Banquo and told him the problem. Blessed went to O'Toole's room and, when the curtain went up to a full house, O'Toole made his entrance dressed in a hastily constructed costume that included jogging trousers and gym shoes. Reporters and critics were convinced he was drunk but, as Forbes makes clear, O'Toole had not touched a drop of alcohol since his surgery.

When the time came for Macbeth to appear on stage with blood on his hands, O'Toole dashed to his quick-change room and, instead of just putting his hands into the bath of blood, he immersed his whole self into it and re-emerged dripping Kensington Gore, uttering, 'This is a sorry sight.' It truly was. The audience were both horrified and hysterical. Forbes knew from that moment the production was doomed.

The media made mincemeat of everyone concerned. Timothy West disowned it publicly. Katharine Hepburn, hearing about the ensuing disaster, phoned Forbes and said, 'If you're going to have a disaster, have a big one.'

The critics tore O'Toole's performance to shreds, which was hardly fair; I saw his *Macbeth* and thought he was brilliant. Yet somehow he took it all very calmly and on the second night he entered the theatre and announced to his co-stars, who were still reeling from the stinging reviews, 'It's all wonderful! This is what the theatre is all about.'

The worst was not over. On that second night a bomb scare emptied the theatre which was full to overflowing. When it was safe to return, the audience filed back in and were treated to as extravagant a *Macbeth* as anyone could hope to see. At the end of that performance, Bryan Forbes felt compelled to walk on stage and make a speech, claiming full responsibility for the performances which had been so viciously attacked by the critics. No one seemed to mind; everyone thoroughly enjoyed the play and all its excesses.

In fact, audiences just kept coming. Every night the auditorium was packed. Some came to admire the play, some out of curiosity. Commercially it was enormously successful but at the end of it O'Toole resigned from the Old Vic, the Arts Council withdrew their much needed grant and the Prospect Theatre Company folded. It may all be coincidence. There are many performances of *Macbeth* that have gone off without a hitch. But you try telling actors that. They are the ones who believe it is cursed.

I recall a conversation with British actress Linda Hayden about various aspects of the occult, and she said:

> Just to say '*Macbeth*' is unthinkable – and I just said it! Robin [Askwith] and I were driving to the theatre one evening where he was doing a play, when we stopped at some traffic lights. I saw this man and said, 'Isn't that Harry?' who's an actor friend of ours whom we hadn't seen for a long time. I wound my window down and called to him. He saw me, then he saw Robin, and we were all overjoyed but couldn't get out of our car. Harry started bashing on the roof of our car with a script he had, shouting our names, and when the lights changed we had to drive on.
>
> That night Robin's play went very badly and, of course, Robin thought the audience was lousy! The next morning Harry phoned, and Robin said, 'After seeing you last night I had the worst audience ever. What was that flaming script you kept bashing the top of the car with?'
>
> And Harry said, '*Macbeth*.'
>
> Robin groaned, 'I might have guessed it.'

*

Bad luck does seem to dog the play and when a series of circumstances occur a conclusion is deduced. But is it the correct conclusion? Most 'theatricals' take no chance and that is why they dare not utter the terrible name of *Macbeth*.

Personally, I have never believed the *Macbeth* curse, even if I did nearly get my nose sliced off during the fight scene. But then, when I stop and go back over this whole chapter again, I have to admit – I may be wrong.

9

Past Lives

Have you ever gone somewhere for what you thought was the first time and felt that you have been there before, perhaps in another life? Have you experienced memories, of living at some time in the past? If so, you may well have no problem accepting the notion of reincarnation and could be easily convinced that you will live again some time in the future. You are in formidable company: Shirley Maclaine, Sylvester Stallone, Faye Dunaway, Glenn Ford and Peter Sellers, to mention a few, all believe they have been reincarnated.

The concept of reincarnation is one that appeals to many, perhaps because the idea of coming back is a preferable option to spending eternity in the grave.

Past lives have seemingly been discovered now in thousands of cases, often through hypnosis in a phenomenen known as past-life regression. Among the subjects who have come to believe they are reincarnated through this technique is the star of innumerable westerns, Glenn Ford.

Regression therapy has been much used since the 1950s when American researcher Morey Bernstein discovered that a hypnosis subject, socialite Virginia Tighe, began speaking as though she were living in eighteenth-century Ireland.

In December 1975, Glenn Ford underwent three hypnosis sessions, each a week apart, during which he was regressed and he recalled five previous lives. In his first life, he was a Christian living in third-century Rome. He remembered being a young man when he was arrested by Roman soldiers and taken to the Colosseum. Given the chance to renounce his Christianity, he refused and was thrown to the lions.

In 1666 he was a young British sailor who experienced the

appalling conditions on the ships of the Royal Navy. He survived scurvy and thirst, storms and precarious duty in the crow's nest, only to die from the Great Plague that was sweeping London.

Next he was a member of the guard of King Louis XIV at the Palace of Versailles, where, at the age of 24, he fell in love with a woman and was killed in a duel over her. Once more his life had ended tragically early.

Next, he was a nineteenth-century Scottish music teacher who taught piano to children. He died at the age of 38 in 1840 from tuberculosis. He came back as a trail boss riding herd for a Denver cattle baron in the late 1800s. Once again his life ended prematurely, this time at the age of 30, when he was killed in an ambush.

Of these regression sessions at the age of 62, he said, 'This has been a somewhat unsettling experience'. If these images really were memories of past lives, then it may account for his chosen career in this life as an actor, especially considering that he is now best remembered as a star of westerns like *3.10 to Yuma*, *The Man from the Alamo* and *Cimarron*, which reflected his last life as a trail boss.

On the other hand, it may be argued that his 'memory' of being a real-life cowboy is merely an image summoned up by his career as a screen cowboy. However, his other 'lives' certainly do not represent his career, since he has never played a Scottish music teacher, a third-century Roman, a guard of Louis XIV or a seventeenth-century sailor.

To understand what regression hypnosis is, I spoke to Elaine Carpenter, a qualified hypnotherapist, whose practice in the depths of Suffolk has produced some remarkable successes in treating people for various disorders, sometimes using regression therapy. In explaining the treatment, she said:

> First, you must understand what hypnotherapy and past-life regression *isn't*. There is the myth that it's tied up with someone taking over minds, and that you go into a magical state. Hypnotherapy has nothing to do with stage hypnotism. It is the use of a trance state which is a naturally

occurring phenomenon and is an ability we all have and use on a daily basis.

For example, day dreaming is a trance state. People can go into a trance while they're driving a car. They drive a familiar route, and they don't remember any of it. What happens is, the conscious mind takes a back seat. Trance can be induced by watching the windscreen wipers, or watching snow come down.

Stage hypnosis is mainly the use of trance for entertainment and appears to look powerful and controlled. Hypnotherapy is the use of a hypnotic trance as part of a therapeautic process. It is a profound state of relaxation, and is also a learned response so each time you have a session you get better at it. I use various methods such as guided relaxation and visualization, such as asking the person to imagine walking down a hill or down steps. It is not successful with everybody. Some people are naturally very deep trance subjects. Most people go into a light to medium trance.

The unconscious mind is like a computer, absorbing memories of sights and sounds. These are all stored in the unconscious mind. The important thing about trance is it gives you better access to these memories. The unconscious mind is suggestible so you can, as a hypnotherapist, put positive ideas into the subject's mind, which is how we help with overcoming anxiety, or giving up smoking, or controlling your diet.

You can also get information out of the unconscious to find the root cause of different problems and this is done through what we call regression. This enables people to remember right back to the earliest days of their lives, including memories from the womb and at birth. In some cases I do what I call a Diagnostic Scan where I get the unconscious mind to indicate at which age the subject experienced the problems. I do this by counting down, all the way to zero if necessary, until the patient's subconscious mind indicates at which age the trouble occurred.

If there is no indication that the problem occurred at any age in this life, I ask the person's subconscious if the problem is associated with a previous life. If this is indicated, I then regress the subject further back.

This is important in the work I do because it may be that the problems people are experiencing are actually traumas which they carry from one life to another. The whole point of going back to that past life is to effect an emotional breakthrough, to allow their feelings out and overcome the fear or trauma that is affecting them in this life.

It is suggested that the most successful of subjects are those with visual creativity and an ability to absorb visual imagery. If so, then it is no wonder that actors are successful at being regressed because their profession is all about visual creativity.

Faye Dunaway discovered her previous lives, not through past-life regression, but through an astrologer. And for this sultry, beautiful woman who shot to fame as one half of *Bonnie and Clyde*, there was one particular aspect to all this, about her original gender, that came as a shock:

> I had some remarkable conversations with an astrologer who went into the subject of reincarnation and, as we talked, she drew out of me things I'd known all the time. Suddenly they came back to me. When I was about 13 I wrote stories. Mysteriously, a language seemed to force itself on me as I wrote in an antiquated English. As this woman pulled it from me, I knew that I wrote plays in seventeenth-century London – and that I was a *man* then.

There is another explanation of Dunaway's memories, based on theories put forward by scientists who reject the idea of reincarnation. In fact, it is one that is suggested in relation to many paranormal incidents: that is, children who experience some form of trauma become extremely sensitive to imagery that may in later life seem real. This may even explain ghost-sighting by children. These images can also be manifested during hypnosis later in life, creating what appear to be memories of alien abduction (of which, more later in the book) and past lives.

It just so happens that Faye Dunaway's parents were divorced when she was 13, leaving her, in her own words, 'a lonely, frightened child'. It was at that age that she began writing stories in ye olde English.

British actress Diane Keene had not been regressed when I met her on the set of the British film *The Shillingbury Blowers* in 1980 but nevertheless she felt that this was not her first time around on this Earth:

> I feel I've lived before. When I was a child I had memories – they weren't dreams – that went back further than one's normal memory. I was riding my bike one day and I suddenly thought, 'I remember the time when me and my friend were riding down here,' and suddenly I remembered something else – from a time long ago. I *remembered* it. I didn't dream it or imagine it.
>
> I began getting these memories when I lived with my parents in Kenya. On the way to and from England we often stopped off in Egypt. The first time in Egypt I had a vivid feeling of having been there before. I found objects in a Cairo museum with which I was somehow familiar. In a temple we visited I felt very uneasy, like I wanted to leave. But something compelled me to stay a long time.
>
> These memories must date back at least a thousand years. I can remember seeing my brother being killed when he was run down by a cart. I've spoken to experts on the subject and they have told me that when one is young, your mind is far more open and if memories are going to come, they come then. The memories usually fade and sometimes return when you're about 45.
>
> I think there is a part of one's mind that is more open, more inert, more developed in some people than in others, so not everybody remembers.
>
> There are theories that you are reincarnated to learn lessons that you didn't learn in previous lives in order to

reach a higher state of grace on the other side. You opt to come back, to be more aware of your faults, so when you go over to the other side you are a better person, or better soul, and you come nearer to 'God'.

Another British star, Oliver Tobias, who sent female hearts racing when he was in *The Stud* and *The Wicked Lady* believes, though is not insistent, that he probably lived in England in a previous life. In this life, he was born to a Swiss father and a German mother, and came to England when he was eight. As soon as he arrived on English shores, he felt he was not a stranger to the isles. He told me, 'It seemed as if I had an affinity with England. It was as though I had been here before. I sensed something even at that young age. The odd thing was, the thought of it, or the memory of it, made me cry all the way from Dover to London. It was almost a rejection or perhaps a fear of something in the past. What that was, I have no idea.'

Sylvester Stallone also believes he has lived before, during the French Revolution and during the British Raj in India.

For some, the very idea of having lived before this life, of having died and come back again, is a serious philosophy that answers many otherwise seemingly unanswerable questions and solves unfathomable mysteries. This is how it was for Shirley Maclaine, one of reincarnation's most passionate defenders. Her realization that she has been reincarnated was only a part of her experience of 'getting in touch with myself', as she put it.

She had begun in show business in 1950 in the chorus of a revival of *Oklahoma!* and made her film debut in 1955 in Hitchcock's *The Trouble with Harry*. By 1960 she was a big star, winning the British Film Academy Award for her performance in *The Apartment*. But she managed to keep her feet firmly on the ground, saying, 'To me stardom was not a goal. It was a by-product. I wanted to do what I was able to do with all my might. To do otherwise seemed not only wasteful but dangerous.'

She also had another philosophy that revealed something of the deep-thinking young mind she had even then. She said, 'My main ambition is to be part of something that's real. I want to make pictures that are an expression of people. I want to tell the truth about life.'

But her problem was, she didn't know the truth. So she went in search of it, and she writes very eloquently about how she did this in a number of books. What she believes she discovered about herself may seem hard to swallow but it is undeniably thought-provoking.

She was told by a friend, Kevin Ryerson, who tunes in to 'spiritual entities', that she was reincarnated at least three times during the 500-year period which, he said, corresponds to the Biblical Garden of Eden. The spiritual entity who imparted this knowledge through Kevin goes by the name of John.

To the cynical and the sceptics, and the plain agnostics like myself, this practice of receiving what Maclaine describes as 'one of the telephones in my life' may be too fantastic a concept to accept readily, but the object of the exercise here is to open the mind and see things the way Shirley Maclaine does. For the more inquisitive minded, I recommend her books. She, of course, is well aware that there are those who will scoff, and in *Out on a Limb* she writes, '... each person experiences his own reality, and no one else can be the judge of what that reality really is.'

According to 'John', this 500-year period was the most spiritually evolved civilization in Earth's history. Maclaine had lived during that period twice as a male and once as a female. According to the 'Akashic records' she was created as a 'twin soul' who knew 'John' because he was her teacher and she his brightest pupil.

If all of Shirley's knowledge of her past lives came through 'John', there would certainly be some doubt over the authenticity of her previous incarnations. But she underwent a process that produced memories of some of these lives, known as 'spiritual acupuncture', not unlike the more conventional method of acupuncture (if, indeed, acupuncture can be called conventional) but which produces a trance-like state similar to regression. Needles were placed in Shirley's throat, shoulders, behind her ears and in her 'third eye'.

As she lay there she began to see images from previous lives. In particular, she saw herself lying on a slab of cement in a state of suspended animation, taking part in some kind of experiment. Apparently she had agreed to leave her body and enter the bodies of other forms, a process which apparently occurred over a period of centuries.

A year after this spiritual acupuncture, she returned to undergo the experience again. In this state she found she had the ability to commune with her 'higher self' and saw herself lying, surrounded by lavender flowers, in a desert, trying to beam light to another soul somewhere in the universe. As she lay on the table with the needles in her, her right arm became painful. Her higher self explained that the other soul in her memory had wanted to depart but Shirley would not allow the other soul to go and held on to that soul with her right arm. But the soul did depart, and the pain of the experience was still being felt.

She went on to see herself in various visions. In one she was dressed in white robes in a marble temple with other people. In another, she was living with elephants, but decided she had to leave them and head for a city. Somehow a fire started and the elephants stampeded towards the city. She was chased by a solitary elephant who blamed her for the fire. As her 'present' self lay on the table seeing all this, she was experiencing a terrible pain in her chest which became intolerable.

As the vision continued, she saw herself on the ground with the elephant crushing her. She did not know why she had left the elephants, only that she loved this particular elephant and now, as she recalled it, her chest and back were in such agony that she could hardly breathe. According to her higher self the elephant was alive again and was looking for her to make peace and to lead her somewhere.

In a further vision , or memory, she saw herself lying on a slab, her body looking as if it was made of stone. White-robed priests lifted her body and carried it to a place of worship, standing the body upright as though she were a stone idol. People were chanting before her. She felt as though she was a false representative of spiritual authority and it was as though this image lasted for centuries. It was all part of her participation in the experiment of soul and body suspension.

She believes this experience helped her to understand why she felt guilty about other people's negativity and why she felt so responsible for the the destiny of so many other people in her current life. She believes that she may have created her present life as a famous film star to enable her to be at the forefront of the New Age spiritual movement.

In time Maclaine began to experience past memories without going through 'John' or spiritual acupuncture. On a visit to an Inca ruin called Ollantaitambo, she found herself with a compulsion to climb the hillside ruin to the top. She used the stone foot ledges to make her way up, and found that she knew exactly where they were. She remembered climbing there before, wearing sandals and some kind of plumage around her neck.

She found this 'the most bewitchingly haunting feeling I had had in a long time' and that it was very different from the past-life regression process under spiritual acupuncture. She just knew that somewhere above was a lookout tower, and she was making her way towards it. It was a place where she felt she had once spent a great deal of time. It became increasingly difficult to breathe at the high altitude but she found she could overcome this by focusing on her past-life experience which she was now reliving, and the breathing difficulty completely vanished.

She climbed into the tower and in an 'altered state' saw priests clad in white, sitting in the lotus position and meditating. They were levitating giant 20-ton stones from the quarries in the valley below up to the site of the temple that was being built. 'I was in sheer and absolute heaven,' she wrote in *It's All in the Playing*.

It is hard to imagine having such experiences, and easy to scoff. But those experiences have marked Shirley Maclaine who remains one of the most thoughtful and talented Hollywood actresses, who finally won an Oscar in 1984 for *Terms of Endearment*.

In 1987, she made a film for CBS based on her book *Out on a Limb*, which traced her journey of self discovery and in which she played herself. *Variety* noted: 'Of course, there's no way of knowing how well she succeeds [playing herself], only how believable she makes it. Not very.'

Peter Sellers also believed he was reincarnated but not in the usual sense of having died and come back as someone else. He said in 1974, 'When I am searching for a character, I leave myself open, as does a medium. And I think that sometimes you can be inhabited by the spirit of someone who lived at sometime, or who was a bit like the person you are doing. And maybe they come in and use you as a chance to relive again.'

One of these spirits was Dan Leno, the clog dancer and Drury Lane pantomime dame. When Sellers was making *The Optimists of Nine Elms*, he wanted to become possessed by Leno, and succeeded – or so he believed. This, perhaps, borders on spirit possession, but Sellers did not think of it in those terms. Said Anthony Simmons who wrote the screenplay, 'He simply felt he was the spirit of Dan Leno reincarnated.' On the set of his penultimate film, *Being There*, Sellers told his co-star Shirley Maclaine that he *knew* all the characters he had played and that he *was* each of those characters at one time or another.

She asked him, 'You mean you feel you are drawing on those experiences and feelings that you actually remember living in other lifetimes?' He said he did, and told her, 'I don't go into this with many people, you know, or they'll think I'm bonkers.' She concluded that he had better past-life recall than most other people she had met.

John Lennon appeared to have been through a number of incarnations, according to Bill Tenuto. He told the medium that he had lived directly before his last birth in '...the south-western portion of China. I don't know what I was; a simple kind of person, perhaps a farmer or a merchant, but not a very wealthy one. I died quite early on.'

He and Yoko Ono had lived together in a past life. 'I was a very strict father to her. She was a rebellious and resentful type of daughter.' Many who believe in reincarnation do accept that we choose to be born again at the same time as those we already know and that, while in some lives we may be married to a partner, in another life that partner may be just a friend, or a relative of some kind. It is, they say, all part of the learning process.

Like Doris Stokes who claimed Lennon told her he was not bitter towards his killer Mark Chapman, Tenuto said that Lennon claimed he and Chapman had lived in a past life in which Lennon shot him in the back. Lennon said he held no rancour towards Chapman who was, after all, only settling an old score.

Now that Lennon has been accepted by the White Brotherhood he no longer needs to be incarnated. Presumably this Earth shall not see him again. We shall see.

American actress Karen Black, who was hugely popular during the late 1960s and throughout the 1970s in such films as *Easy Rider*, *Five Easy Pieces*, *Capricorn One* and *Airport 1975*, believes she has lived several times before. In one life she was an aristocratic Frenchwoman and, in another life, a wandering, lusty and unfaithful husband.

'I make no apologies for my belief in reincarnation,' she said. 'After all, half the world believes in it, but people won't admit it for fear of being ridiculed.'

That is an interesting point and it does seem that today more and more people are accepting the possibility. However, while one should never close one's mind, one should not forget that in recent years people have been made victims of a phenomenon known as False Memory Syndrome. Not that this means that all people who have been regressed have false memories, but it does mean that there are some unscrupulous hypnotherapists cashing in on the misery of those who seek help. For the record, Elaine Carpenter, under whom I have had hypnotherapy, is not one of them. At the very least, while I have not had regression, I can vouch for the very real benefits of hypnotherapy.

Going back to what Diane Keene said about children having

these memories, I recall having what may or may not have been a childhood memory in which I wondered what it was like to die. Being a child, I reasoned that being dead had to be like it was before being born. I seemed to be able to recall what it was like before birth, although now I can recall little more than having a feeling of existing then in some form or another. But whether this is an actual memory or a childhood fantasy, I honestly cannot say.

Lindsay Wagner, *The Bionic Woman* in the 1970s TV series, has a remarkable memory, perhaps not too unlike my own, but one that has remained vivid to her. She can recall a time before she was born, when she was in her mother's womb. She could recall that her parents went to see a film while her mother was pregnant. Her mother kept crying during the movie and her father kept going to the back of the cinema to talk about sport to an old friend.

If Wagner's memory is a true memory, than perhaps it is also true that the unconscious mind is, as Elaine Carpenter told me, like a computer, storing all these memories which have to be accessed. And in this way, past lives may be recalled. However, not every hypnotherapist believes memories necessarily indicate a past life. Dr Marge Reider, a researcher into hypnotic regression in Lake Elsinore, California, where she has regressed many subjects, has herself undergone regressive hypnosis and relived a past life as a nurse living in Millboro after the Civil War. Yet she has found by regressing two sets of identical twins and one set of identical triplets that each of the twins and triplets seemed to relive the same past life as their brothers and sisters.

Dr Reider reasons that if they had been reincarnated, how could the soul of a single person from the past life now split into two or three souls and so inhabit genetically linked but individual bodies? She suggests that there may be a genetic memory link, which supports theories by researchers who favour the idea of genetically inherited memories. Not everyone who believes in reincarnation has actually lived before. For some it is a matter of faith and belief. Indian star Persis Khambatta, who shot to fame as the sexy but bald Deltan in *Star Trek: The Motion*

Picture, told me, 'I believe that if I do wrong in this life I will pay for it eventually. I suppose that's why I believe in reincarnation. I haven't lived before. But I might live again. A spiritualist once told me that I have a new soul. I want to be a good, happy soul.'

Personally, the idea of having battled my way through this life only to find I've got to come back and go through birth, life and death yet again, presumably until I get it right, does not endear itself to me.

10

Close Encounters

In 1950, Hollywood was treated to a startling revelation about a UFO, care of Frank Scully, a reporter on Hollywood's *Weekly Variety*. His job usually dealt only with the ins and outs of the movie business but in 1950 he wrote a book, *Behind the Flying Saucers*, which alleged that 'the first saucer to land on this earth' crashed east of Aztec, New Mexico, in 1948. He alleged that 16 dead aliens were found. They were three-and-a-half feet long and, apart from unusually pointed features, resembled humans.

The flying saucer, which was 99 feet in diameter, was dismantled and removed to the top-secret Hangar 18 in Wright-Patterson AFB in Dayton, Ohio, reported Scully. Unfortunately, Scully's report was investigated by reporter JP Cahn in 1952 and he revealed that Scully had received most of his information from two con men who had been arrested in 1952 for trying to sell worthless war-surplus equipment and oil-detection devices.

It was thought that their 'research' was actually based on an incident on 2 July 1947, when a 'flying disc' was said to have crashed at Roswell, New Mexico. The bodies of aliens had been removed from the wreckage to be examined; one alien was said to still be alive. But the US Army Air Force announced that what they had first called a 'flying disc' was actually a weather balloon. Then the Air Force announced that the weather balloon was actually highly classified radiation detection experiment. The Aztec UFO turned out to be a proven hoax, although author Frank Scully seems to have been unwitting in his involvement since he paid the two con men for their story.

These accounts captured the imagination of countless Americans. One in particular was Jackie Gleason.

Few comedy actors came bigger than Jackie Gleason. To call him a heavyweight was, to him, no insult for, like many a successful comedian with more than the average waist size, he used his hefty physique to his own advantage.

But his gift for making people laugh did not prevent him from taking a serious interest in a subject which was taboo in a town where it was far more normal to divorce and marry at leisure, indulge in drugs and alcohol just to be sociable, and spend money like it was going out of fashion. The taboo subject was little green men from outer space; at least, that's how most people looked upon it. Rational-thinking people did not believe that men came from Mars in flying saucers. That was purely the realm of fantasy, reserved for Buck Rogers and Flash Gordon. Anyone who thought otherwise might well find themselves certified and put in an institution. So for years Jackie Gleason kept his interest in the subject of UFOs and life on other planets to himself.

How he came to regard the subject as something worth expending time and energy on might be ascribed to the broken home of his childhood. Born in Brooklyn, New York in 1916, he was brought up without a father, who went absent probably before Gleason could even remember him. So Gleason, brought up during the years of the depression, had no one to make him go to school each day. Instead he got his education in the local pool halls, preparing himself for his role in the 1961 classic film *The Hustler*, in which he was the big-time pool player challenged by hustler Paul Newman.

At the tender age of 15, young Gleason entered a talent contest as a comedian, and won. He was soon performing in vaudeville, carnivals and night clubs until, in 1940, he was signed by Warner Brothers to a film contract. He played character parts in numerous films, appeared on Broadway and then switched between playing drama and comedy.

Then he heard about the 'flying disc' that landed at Roswell in New Mexico in 1947. Like a few others, Gleason's interest was alerted. He had no great desire to investigate the matter for himself but he wondered about what seemed an attempt to cover up whatever happened at Roswell. It ignited his curiosity about the possibility of other life in outer space.

Then came the Frank Scully story. Many scoffed, and even when that story was proved to be untrue, Gleason kept an open mind. Over the years, reports of flying saucers, as they came to be known, continued to keep Americans interested in the UFO phenomenon. Gleason, who never claimed to see a UFO, remained fascinated and wondered, like so many others, why the army, who seemed to be responsible for investigating UFOs, denied their existence. But it was not a subject that could be discussed openly by a Hollywood celebrity...

It was during the 1950s and into the 1960s that Gleason established his popularity on television in *The Life of Riley*, *The Honeymooners* and *The Jackie Gleason Show*. During the 1960s Gleason's film career really took off, with films such as *Gigot* which he also wrote, and *Requiem for a Heavyweight*. Through his success in films and on TV he became, like many Hollywood actors (although he actually lived in Florida), acquainted with important politicians. He found a firm friend in Richard Nixon.

In 1973, when Nixon was president of the United States, Gleason tried to find out from him the truth about UFOs. He wanted to know if they really existed and if the army was involved in a cover up that came from the very top. Nixon put through a few phone calls and before long, Gleason was being whisked off to Homestead Air Base in Florida with strict instructions that what he was to be shown was top secret.

He arrived amid great secrecy. Everything seemed to have been carefully arranged for his visit. Armed guards escorted him to a building at a remote area on the vast site. What he saw astounded him. Laid out were four embalmed bodies. They were two feet long, each with a small head and large ears. He knew they were not human but when he asked his escorts exactly what they were and where they came from, he was told that the information was classified.

He arrived back at his Florida home and, shortly after, his wife Beverly returned to find him quite shaken. She asked him what was wrong and he told her of the day's events, swearing her to total secrecy.

However, some years later when she and Gleason divorced,

she wrote of the Homestead Air Base incident in a book. That book was never published for some reason, but news of Gleason's aliens story became an open secret which he refused to discuss. One ufologist, who in the mid 1980s was attempting to sue the US government to get it to reveal its UFO secrets, heard of Gleason's story and of his ex-wife's unpublished book. He tried to persuade Jackie Gleason to tell his story in court. Gleason flatly refused, so the ufologist tried to subpoena him. He failed, and Gleason kept quiet to the day he died in 1987.

It is easy to forget that Ronald Reagan was an actor long before he became president of the United States of America. He actually started out as a radio sportscaster, reporting on the Chicago Cubs baseball games before being signed by Warner Brothers in 1937. He went on to play leads in some 50 films, most of them B movies but some were memorable, such as *King's Row* and *The Hasty Heart*.

He served as a captain with the American Army Air Force during the Second World War, making training films. Once peace was declared, he became involved in the politics of the film industry: it was the beginning of what was to become an increasingly political career.

He was elected president of the Screen Actors Guild in 1947 and served until 1952. He was good at it too and was reinstated in 1959 when he was instrumental in negotiating some important new terms between actors and studios. He continued to make films, including the memorable Don Siegel thriller *The Killers* in 1964. But he was gradually being drawn into political activity and, in 1966, he emerged as the Republican governor of California, serving for eight years.

One night in 1974, Governor Reagan was aboard a Cessna Citation aircraft that was approaching Bakersfield in California when he and his two security guards saw an object flying just to their rear.

Pilot Bill Paynter recalled, 'It appeared to be several hundred yards away. It was a fairly steady light until it began to accelerate. Then it appeared to elongate. Then the light took off. It went up at a 45-degree angle – at a high rate of speed. Everyone on the plane was surprised.'

No one on board knew exactly what they were looking at but what they did agree was they had observed a UFO. 'The UFO went from a normal cruise speed to a fantastic speed instantly,' said Paynter. 'If you give an aeroplane power, it will accelerate, but not like a hot-rod, and that's what this was like.'

The story may have remained a secret matter between Reagan and the others but for Norman C Miller, the Washington bureaux chief for the *Wall Street Journal*. A week after the sighting, Reagan was talking to Miller and, surprisingly, Reagan brought up the subject of the UFO. 'We followed it for several minutes,' Reagan told him. 'It was a bright white light. We followed it to Bakersfield, and all of a sudden to our utter amazement it went straight up into the heavens.'

Miller expressed his doubts that Reagan had seen a flying saucer of any kind and at that point, according to Miller, the governor suddenly remembered that he was talking to a reporter and 'a look of horror came over him'. Reagan promptly changed the subject.

Since then Reagan has not discussed the incident publicly but it is known that during his term as president he became increasingly interested in UFOs and looked into the secret investigations that the US military were conducting into the whole subject. But under his administration no UFO secrets were ever revealed.

When Shirley Maclaine was in Peru filming *Out on a Limb*, she found that almost everyone who lived there had a story to tell about UFOs. Anton Ponce de Leon, a cultural anthropologist responsible for investigating UFO sightings in Cuzco, told her of a night he was driving home along a mountain road and saw a string of lights hovering over a lagoon. He got out of the car to investigate and discovered the UFO, or UFOs, made no sound; he could not tell if the lights were made by one object or several. The two ends of the string of lights linked up to form a circle. Another light appeared over the city of Cuzco, moving towards the circle, until it hovered over Anton who then saw clearly that this single light was a giant craft. It linked up with the other lights and remained like that for the next few hours. Anton observed it until he grew too cold.

He told Maclaine, 'After that, I no longer called anyone else crazy for what they reported. And those who call me crazy now will stop after they have their own experience.'

Maclaine had become aware of the UFOs during an earlier stay in Peru when an old woman, who was cooking in the small hotel where Shirley was staying, told her that she had seen many UFOs, as had her uncle who was frightened when he first saw one fly into Lake Titicaca and disappear. She told Maclaine, 'He thought maybe he was going loco. But then several of his friends told him they had seen the same thing. He felt better.'

The woman said that the extra-terrestrials live high in the mountains. 'They fly their discs way under the mountains so that no one can find them.'

Maclaine learned that the people there were so used to seeing UFOs that they wondered why she and others were so intrigued. They laughed at the astronomers who came in the hope of studying them because the local people knew the UFOs would never appear when the astronomers were watching. The 'disc people', as they called them, liked to be alone, and so the locals left them alone. Nobody in the mountains had ever been hurt by the 'disc people' – and Maclaine concluded that the extra-terrestrials were here to do good, and might even be the angels of the Bible.

One man from the old Yugoslavia, who had had a close encounter, told Maclaine that an alien had said to him, 'We want nothing for ourselves. That is our creed where we come from. We do everything for others.'

If this is truly the purpose of aliens in visiting our planet, then perhaps there is some credence to Bill Tenuto's claim that John Lennon revealed to him, 'There are thousands of friendly aliens from many different galaxies, many of whom are on the Earth at the present time in various forms and disguises to help us out of our most dire circumstances. There are many of them walking around as human beings which we think are human beings but are really UFOs in disguise.'

UFOs in disguise? He meant aliens, of course. Even a spirit working with the White Brotherhood can presumably make a slip of the tongue.

In recent years tales of people being abducted by aliens have become quite common. But the true estimate of just how many people have experienced this – assuming it is a real phenomenon – is unknown because too many people fear ridicule. One person who has allowed his story to be told is Michael Bershad, the popular American TV actor.

He used to suffer an irrational feeling of dread for years every time he travelled on a particular stretch of Route 40 near his home. Early in 1978 he went to see hypnotherapist George Fisher. Fisher had been trained by psychiatrist Bob Naiman who specialized in regressing abductees. Under hypnosis, Bershad recalled driving along the highway one night in 1973 and suddenly finding that his car had been pulled over to the hard shoulder. He then found himself out of the car, being approached by dark figures who placed a large brass-like clamp on his shoulder. The clamp prevented him from moving voluntarily.

Above was a bright light. In his trance state, Bershad said, 'It's day, but it's night.' He came out of the trance in a state of severe stress.

Later that year he underwent a further hypnosis session under therapist Aphrodite Clamar who also had a number of clients who were possible abductees. She took Bershad back to that night in 1973 when he was driving along Route 40. This time he recalled seeing two lights above him as he was driving. The lights disappeared into a wood and he pulled over and got out of the car. Three beings approached him. Their heads were oversized with faces that were a sort of putty-white, harbouring large glistening eyes. Their feet were shaped like large almonds. One of them began digging a hole in the ground next to the car. Bershad could remember no more.

In 1980 he had another session with Clamar and this time he recalled the clamp on the shoulder, and remembered that it was connected to a saucer-shaped craft that had landed. He was led up a ramp to the craft and went inside. He recalled walking around inside for a while and then found himself on a table in a round, white room. A contraption, not unlike a big old dentists' drill, came down from the ceiling. Something dug into his back, causing him great pain and moving his legs in a frog-like manner. A small cylinder, like a small tube, was pressed into his stomach. His legs were lifted into stirrups and he was examined further.

Bershad was later questioned by a Brooklyn neurologist, Paul Cooper, and from the description of the way his legs moved, Cooper concluded that the movement would result from a probe stimulating the femoral nerve in the spinal cord.

A keen Hollywood investigator of UFOs is screen writer Tracy Tormé, the son of singer Mel Tormé. His investigations have led to his reputation as something of an expert on the subject of both UFOs and abductions. In 1982 he met David Jacobs, one of America's leading authorities on UFOs and a healthy sceptic of many of the stories about UFOs and alien abductions.

Tormé wanted to speak to Jacobs about the possibility of a government conspiracy to cover up the UFO phenomenon. They met at an apartment in New York which was owned by Universal Studios, and went for a walk through Central Park while Tormé urged Jacobs to meet Budd Hopkins, an artist who, with his wife and a friend, had seen a UFO over Route 6 in 1964. Hopkins reported that it was a metallic-looking object which performed high-speed manoeuvres. When Hopkins reported the sighting to Otis Air Force Base, he was met by an unwillingness to shed light on the subject.

He became interested in the UFO phenomenon but concentrated on his work until a friend revealed that he had been abducted by aliens. Hopkins investigated his friend's story with TV actor Ted Bloecher, another UFO enthusiast, and they managed to find an apartment doorman who had reported seeing his friend's UFO to the police. That convinced Hopkins and Bloecher that this was one UFO abduction story that was true.

Hopkins wrote a story for the *Village Voice* newspaper entitled SANE CITIZEN SEES UFO IN NEW JERSEY. After its publication, a woman contacted Hopkins and Bloecher with her own story of alien abduction. Bloecher found the story too much for him and he told the woman, 'You've gone past the limit of my belief. I don't believe a word you're saying.' Both Hopkins and Bloecher were interested only in authentic stories and found they had to sift through the science-fiction fantasies as other people claiming to be abductees came forward. Bloecher and Hopkins often disagreed over the authenticity of the stories. But they became known as serious investigators of alien abduction.

David Jacobs agreed to meet Hopkins, and Tracy Tormé took him to a house where Hopkins and a few other abductees awaited him. Jacobs had harboured reservations about many of the cases Hopkins had investigated, but they did agree that the Earth was being visited by aliens of an advanced intelligence for unknown reasons.

One of Hopkins' abductee contacts was Michael Bershad, a close friend of Ted Bloecher. The two actors and Tracy Tormé represented a small group of Hollywood professionals who were serious UFO investigators but regarded as cranks by many of their peers.

Budd Hopkins continued his investigations and in due course he received a phone call from Whitley Strieber, a successful writer, whose books *The Wolfen* and *The Hunger* had been made into films. He had become a part of Hollywood society, although he lived in New York. He had begun to feel an inexplicable anxiety about living New York after an incident in the autumn of 1985. He met Hopkins to tell his story.

Strieber, with his wife, Anne, their son Andrew, and their writer friends Annie Gottlieb and Jacques Sandulescu, had gone to the Striebers' upstate house in the woods. That evening something tripped the outside lights and the burglar alarm went off. Andrew screamed that something was in his room but, when

Strieber rushed in, all he found was a spider on the table. Andrew told him, 'It might not have been a spider that I saw.'

After the household had settled down to sleep, the outside lights went on again. Strieber investigated downstairs but found nothing and returned to his room. However, instead of going to bed he sat in a chair and watched as the door opened slightly, revealing what appeared to be a large, glistening eye. He thought he was hallucinating. Suddenly the house was bathed in light from above. A small being came into the room, walked up to Strieber and held what appeared to be a luminous wand to his forehead. Strieber felt he was no longer in control of himself but, hearing Andrew scream, he managed to knock the wand away and run to his son's bedroom where the terrified boy told him that something was in his room.

Strieber thought that while he was hallucinating, Andrew was just having a nightmare. Anne had slept through it all but Annie Gottlieb and Jacques Sandulescu were woken by the light. The following morning they insisted that Strieber take them back to Manhattan. From that night on Strieber grew more anxious about New York, and he finally told his wife that he wanted to move to his home state of Texas. They put their Manhattan apartment and their upstate house on the market and moved in to a house in Austin, Texas. Then he developed a phobia about the sky over Austin and decided he did not want to live there after all. He seemed to be falling apart and Anne threatened him with divorce if he did not pull himself together. They moved back to New York and at Christmas went back to their unsold upstate house in the woods, as had been their tradition.

On 26 December, at around eleven in the evening, he was woken by a whooshing sound coming from the living room. He tried to go back to sleep but saw that the bedroom door was moving. A small creature appeared, about three and a half feet high with large black eyes. It wore a smooth round hat and a breastplate etched with concentric circles. It rushed at Strieber and the next thing he knew he was floating naked out of the room.

He next found himself out in the woods, sitting opposite a

small figure in a grey-tan body suit. Next to him stood another being, possibly a female, who was doing something to the side of his head. Then he was launched into the air, flying past the branches of the trees, and found himself in a circular chamber, where four different kinds of beings attended to him. One of them put a needle into his head which made him fall back. They inserted something into his rectum and colon, an incision was made in his right forefinger, and then he blacked out.

He came to back in his bed. His rectum was sore. For two days he suffered extreme anxiety and tried to overcome it by writing a story called *Pain*, in which he is imprisoned and tortured by a female demon. In the story he emerges with a new insight into the world and a spiritual strength.

But it did not exorcize his anxiety as he had hoped. Finally he allowed himself to consider a possibility he had been resisting: that he might have been abducted by aliens. So he contacted Bud Hopkins.

After listening to his story, Hopkins told Strieber that he ought to see a psychiatrist, and before long Strieber was being seen by Don Klein, the director of the New York State Psychiatric Institute, and undergoing regression therapy.

He recalled, in different sessions, how a female alien had tried to get him to achieve an erection, telling him, 'You are our chosen one.' He begged that he would wake and find it was all a dream and the next moment he was back in the lounge of his house in the woods, naked.

On another occasion, he was taken in the space craft and saw a group of soldiers who were laid out in what appeared to be a coma. His own father was there, standing over Strieber's sister who lay sprawled on a table in her nightgown. Their father was looking down at her with an expression of frozen surprise.

Despite these emerging memories, the Striebers returned from time to time to the house. One night he awoke to feel paralysed while a probe was pushed up his nose and into his brain. After this he developed nose bleeds, as did both Anne and Andrew. He also experienced episodes of missing time.

As the therapy under Don Klein continued, Strieber sought a

medical diagnosis for his disorders. He had neurological examinations and scans of his temporal lobes. Nothing conclusive was discovered to explain his paranoia or anxiety and what might still be just fantasies. He finally came to accept the likelihood that he had been the victim of alien abduction.

Strieber began writing about his experiences in his famous book, *Communion*, and later in screenplay form for the film version which Strieber produced. In the film he was played by Christopher Walken.

However, Hopkins became sceptical about Strieber's abduction experiences and when he read the first draft of *Communion* he felt that much of it originated from Strieber, the writer of horror books rather than from Strieber, the abductee. He urged Strieber to abandon the draft he had written and to wait until his therapy had been completed before attempting to write it again. But Strieber felt that Hopkins's criticisms were an attempt at censorship and went ahead to find a publisher. The book was published in January 1987, and sold several million copies worldwide. Its success spawned the film version in 1990.

During the final stages of writing the book, in April 1986, Strieber was at his house in the woods when he awoke to find himself in the corridor of a spaceship. Two of the aliens led him to a room which resembled a British regimental mess in India during the Raj. He was asked why the British empire had collapsed and he gave them a lengthy answer. Later he was shown a drawer in which alien bodies lay inert in cellophane. He woke up in his own room.

The next night he woke up and went to his son's room to discover Andrew had disappeared. Strieber went outside and saw a dark spaceship and some aliens who told him to go back to his room. He did so, and the next morning he found Andrew safe and well. The boy began saying some unusual things: 'You know, I've been thinking. Reality is God's dream.' Later he noted, 'The unconscious mind is like the universe out beyond the quasars. It's a place we want to go to find out what's there.' Apparently, Strieber and his family have learned to live with their unearthly visitors.

Bud Hopkins, David Jacobs and Tracy Tormé went on to write the four-hour mini-series *Intruders*, based on Hopkins's book about a series of foetus-snatchings he and David Jacobs had investigated. It went out on American television in 1992.

Another screen writer who turned his own close encounters into a screen story is Jerico Stone. But there was little to compare in his original screenplay, based on what he insists are true experiences, to the 1988 Kim Bassinger comedy *My Stepmother Is an Alien*.

He began to write his script, not so much as an alien encounter story but as an 'allegory about child abuse'. He told Patrick Goldstein of *Empire* magazine that, as a kid in Brooklyn, he was frequently 'beaten up' and took refuge by spending his days in a railway station, reading comics with a black boy who was also the victim of abuse.

They fantasized about being super-heroes and called themselves the Black Jacks. 'It gave us strength,' said Jerico. But one day his friend turned up having been badly beaten and said that nothing could be done to stop his father because he was an alien. 'He said he couldn't see me again,' said Jerico, 'and he never did.'

Some years later Jerico made his way to Los Angeles where he lived on the streets and slept in parks, and made friends with another black boy. One day his friend turned up badly beaten, and told Jerico that it was his father who had beaten him. But, he said, he couldn't fight back because his father was an alien.

The black boy returned to a supermarket car park to meet his father in an old abandoned car. Jerico followed, and saw the boy get into the car. Jerico recalled, 'It didn't have any wheels and its windows were spray-painted black. I started kicking the car door, when the door opened and . . . it was an alien. It wasn't a man. It looked so strange, I couldn't even describe it.'

He told *Empire* that suddenly a huge hand leaped out and dug into his stomach, 'grabbing hold of my spine. The pain was so intense I collapsed.'

The alien stood over him and said, very gently, 'Sorry, Black Jack'.

'The car started to shimmer, very brightly,' said Jerico, 'and I blacked out from the pain. When I came to, the car – and any traces of it – was gone.'

There is a growing conviction among some investigators that many claims of alien abduction are a direct result of suffering child abuse. It is a theory that is applied to virtually all forms of paranormal experience. Seeing ghosts, poltergeists, past-life memories and alien abduction have been put down to traumatic childhoods. If true, then Jerico Stone's story certainly sounds like such a case. But in this instance, he did not publicly admit to this tale until 1989, a year after he saw his screenplay, which was intended as a horror film about child abuse, turned into a comedy that flopped badly at the box office.

The original screen story was, said Jerico, 'a fable, a fairy tale that would make it easier for kids to grasp the child abuse angle'. It told of a child's nightmarish vision that his stepmother was an evil alien who violently abuses him. But no one believes him because, in public, she's the greatest mother in the world. 'It was,' said Jerico, 'a very dark story.'

He says he was inspired to write the screenplay after meeting Orson Welles who told him, 'My boy, *The War of the Worlds* was just a dress rehearsal.'

Guy Rydell, who was an executive at New Line Cinema when the project went to them, said, 'I thought it would have made a great horror picture. I was terribly saddened to hear that they turned it into a comedy.' Another studio executive who read it found it to be 'a very real, terrifying story'.

In Hollywood Jerico is viewed as something of a renegade and, said one development executive who has had a series of meetings with him, 'a real weirdo'. Producer Tony Deutsch said, 'He does have a very strange lifestyle. I don't think he's gone to sleep before dawn since he was a kid.'

In 1980 I had the good fortune to interview Arthur C Clarke who was, and perhaps remains, arguably the most respected of all science-fiction writers. His screenplay for *2001: A Space Odyssey*, written in collaboration with Stanley Kubrick, suggests that there is intelligent life out there, and I wanted to know if he believed in UFOs. He said:

> The one thing I am reasonably sure about UFOs is that they are not spaceships. I have observed so many UFOs that I wouldn't bother to cross the street to see one today. Every Unidentified Flying Object I've seen has turned out to be an *Identified* Flying Object. Almost every one I saw would fool the layman, and I think I can consider I have some expertise on this subject. The last one I saw was one of the best. I was standing in the shadow of my Colombo house, pointing out the planet Venus to a friend of mine, and I pointed and said, 'There she is.'
>
> My friend pointed to the sky and said, 'No, *there* she is.' We argued about it and finally I began to believe I had discovered that Venus had an identical twin and thought it could be called Supernova Clark. But when I looked through my telescope I discovered it was a meteorological balloon. And it so happens that Venus and weather balloons are often mistaken for UFOs. So if I could mistake a balloon for Venus, then the layman can be forgiven for believing the balloon to be a UFO.
>
> I'd like to see UFOs neglected for a decade and concentrate on the reports of actual close encounters which either occur or do not. There is certainly a lot of high-powered lying and hysterical self-delusion going on. As I always say, time will tell.

Of course, as a pure layman I feel I ought to defer to the man who knows more about any of this than I ever will. But he did say all this back in 1980 and the fact is, UFOs have not gone away or been neglected for a decade, or even for five minutes, and there has been much debate about alien abductions. Those who make these claims, including Whitley Strieber, have described their abductors. These descriptions are not in harmony with Arthur C Clarke's thoughts on how aliens would appear. He said he cannot tell us what aliens would look like but, 'I will tell you what they do not look like. We now understand the principles of human evolution. We are the product of thousands of successive throws of the genetic dice – any one of which might have turned out differently. If the terrestrial experiment started all over again at Time Zero, there might still be intelligence on this planet – but it wouldn't look like us. In the dance of the DNA spirals, the same partners would never meet again.'

So if there is life out there somewhere, its DNA dance should have produced a species that looks very different from us. The aliens who walk the earth who look like us then, cannot exist. Aliens who are humanoid must be figments of the imagination. If Clarke is correct.

In his 1987 book *Chronicles of the Strange and Mysterious*, Clarke wrote that there continues to be no hard evidence that the Earth has ever been visited from space and he cites the fact that the US, the USSR (as it was) and China would know immediately if there were real spaceships. He reasons that it is unlikely that all three powers would 'instantly co-operate to suppress the news'.

Clarke tells a story about a friend of his who used to be deputy director of the CIA who has since gone on to 'a much bigger job'. He called together the CIA's top scientists and asked them to tell him the truth about UFOs. They gave him two answers. They think that there is probably life out there in space. There is not the slightest firm evidence that it has ever visited the Earth.

Despite this assurance from Clarke's CIA friend, the Roswell 'flying disc' incident of 1947 refuses to go away because there are witnesses still living who maintain that they saw the wreckage and the bodies. The US government continue to insist that the wreckage was not a flying saucer, nor were there any alien bodies. However, at the time of the crash, it was the Air Force who told the press that the wreckage was a 'flying disc'.

Now Steven Spielberg is said to be secretly planning a film, called *Project X*, which will expose a cover-up over Roswell. There has been, it is said, a team at Hamlin Productions working on the script since 1993, and the film is due for release in 1997, on the 50th anniversary of the 'alien landing'.

Concurrently, Tracy Tormé is writing a screenplay about Roswell. Whether he is working in collaboration with Spielberg or not cannot be confirmed as the Roswell film is as secret as the incident itself.

But was there really a cover-up or is it all fanciful science fiction? Well, American congressman Steven H Schiff, the representative for New Mexico, is not satisfied with the official version:

> We've had three different explanations from the military about the crash. The first explanation is that it was a flying disc, meaning flying saucer in today's terminology. They changed that and said, 'We made a mistake. It wasn't a flying disc. It was a weather balloon.' I still find it amazing that the United States top bomber wing – the only wing that was eligible to carry nuclear weapons at that particular time – would not know a weather balloon from a flying saucer, but apparently somebody didn't according to them. So we had the second explanation that this was a weather balloon, and we now have the third explanation that it was part of a highly classified radiation detection experiment. So we have three separate explanations as to what crashed but no dispute that something crashed.

Congressman Schiff has discussed with the general accounting office, which oversees government operations, the possibility of releasing the records, if any exist, to the public so people can draw their own conclusions. The GAO did investigate government agencies to establish if any records on Roswell existed and in July 1995 they reported that the Air Force had destroyed its records of the incident.

When Steven Spielberg made his UFO epic, *Close Encounters of the Third Kind*, he engaged the services of Dr J Allen Hynek, considered by many to be the world's leading ufologist. He was appointed the astronomical consultant to the United States Air Force in 1948, a year after Roswell. His investigations led to what was known as 'Project Blue Book' in 1949. Years later he was very critical of the Air Force's methods and conclusions. He claimed that genuine UFO landings took place at Cannon Air Force Base, New Mexico on 18 May 1954, at Deerwood Nike Base on 29 September 1957, and at Blaine Air Force Base on 12 June 1965.

Hynek set up the Independent Center for UFO Studies in 1973 and, while he has no hard and fast theory as to the nature of UFOs, he believes wholeheartedly that they are real and that solving the mystery would be a 'quantum leap' in our understanding.

The title, *Close Encounters of the Third Kind*, was taken from one of four terms which Hynek himself coined to describe UFO contact. Close encounters of the first kind are UFO sightings at close range. The second kind are UFO sightings at close range accompanied by tangible evidence. The third kind are close-up sightings of UFOs and aliens. The fourth kind are alien encounters – or abductions.

Since the break up of the Soviet Union, the Russians have become more open about their UFO sightings and research is being conducted by leading military figures. The army have actually made public film and tape footage of UFOs, after years of the Communist regime forbidding anyone to admit publicly to any UFO experience. Although kept secret from the rest of the world at the time, the former Soviet Union conducted a state-funded programme of UFO research that involved around six million troops as observers.

The denials continue from our democratic governments. The British Ministry of Defence deny that UFOs were seen by American Air Force personnel and local people at Woodbridge in Suffolk in 1980, despite the testimonies of the witnesses concerned, and the US government continues to maintain that no flying saucer crashed at Roswell in 1947, contrary to all the eye-witness reports.

Long after the book that proved to be a false report of a UFO landing by Frank Scully, another Scully has become the hero – or rather heroine – of UFO enthusiasts. But this Scully is a purely fictitious character, the female half of the double act of FBI agents investigating *The X Files*. These television tales of Fox 'Spooky' Mulder and his sceptical sidekick Dana Scully who specialize in paranormal cases, including UFOs, ghosts, military cover-ups, even potential life forms living in America's sewers, has become hugely successful since its first episode in 1993. The motto of the series is 'The truth is out there'.

The series has put its two new stars, David Duchovny and Gillian Anderson, into the international spotlight, and everybody wants to know if they actually believe the kind of things they investigate and pursue on screen. Ironically, Gillian, whose character Scully is the disbelieving one, says, 'I'm much more of a believer than Scully. I believe in UFOs and life on other planets. I also believe in Extra Sensory Perception and in people who can foresee the future.' Gillian, however, bases her beliefs on second-hand stories as she has never seen a UFO herself or had a psychic experience.

On the other hand, Duchovny, whose character in the series is searching for his sister who was abducted by aliens, says, after being asked for the fiftieth time if he believes in aliens, 'For the fiftieth time, no, I do not believe in extra-terrestrials. Unfortunately, Gillian and I have been indoors for eighteen hours a day for the last two years, so we've never seen any aliens.'

The show's creator, Chris Carter, is a student of 'weird science fiction'. He wants to know about everything that has a bizarre twist to it and, if it has a ring of truth to it, it is likely to end up in *The X Files*. The pilot episode was based on documented evidence about teenagers who had suffered alien abduction. Since the advent of the series, even more interest in the paranormal has surfaced.

The whole subject of UFOs, and the regularity with which they are reported, is said to coincide with the release of films, books and television shows. After *Close Encounters of the Third Kind* was released in 1977, a spate of UFO sightings was reported. When *Communion* was published, people began coming forward with horror stories of alien abduction. Sceptics point to this as being something that proves people are influenced by what they see or read and their imagination does the rest. *The X Files* has increased reports. Or perhaps it has increased awareness. It is possible that people refrain from making their experiences known for fear of ridicule until a successful film or book influences their decision to talk about it.

If you happen to be a successful movie star, you are going to think three times, at least, before putting your career on the line by claiming that you saw a flying saucer. Let me take you back at this point to the set of *Damien – Omen II* in 1977, where William Holden was talking about there being 'more things in heaven and earth – and all that'.

In discussing the mysteries of life, he asked me, almost casually, 'Have you ever seen a UFO?'

I told him that I thought I had, just once and very briefly, while standing on a hill in Thornton Heath in Surrey. In the distance I saw something hovering in the sky. Suddenly it went up into the clouds at tremendous speed and that was that.

'Was it at night?' he asked. I told him it was during the day. I could not describe it as disc- or saucer-shaped because it appeared so briefly. What *did* strike me was that it seemed to glow, or perhaps shine. That is what made it visible for probably no more than three or four seconds. He nodded gravely but knowingly. He wanted to know if what I saw was something I considered to be 'of this Earth'. I confessed I had no real idea; it was actually difficult to accept that it might have been something from another world. He wanted to know why I felt this way. I said it was because I did not want to feel like a fool, which is how I assumed others would perceive me. I had therefore said very little about the incident.

Again he nodded gravely and said, 'There was a flying object that crashed in a place called Roswell in 1947. It was supposedly a flying saucer which the Air Force tried to hush up. I guess you can account for a lot of UFOs being weather balloons and some being outright hoaxes. But how do you explain seeing one without everyone thinking you're out of your mind or having the Air Force tell you it never happened?'

For a while I wondered if he was intimating that he had seen the Roswell crash. So I asked him if he had. He shook his head:

We were making a movie – a western – *The Streets of Laredo* – in Arizona. I'm sitting on a rock in between takes. It's a clear sky. William Bendix is lying down with his hat over his eyes, trying to sleep. I'm looking up in the sky – it was clear blue – and I see this ... thing. It's hovering. It looks kind of round, not like a plane or a helicopter. Then it's flying through the sky so fast; I hardly had time to get a good look at it. I nudged Bendix and said, 'See that?' He looked up, squinted, saw something, but it was gone. He said, 'What was that?' I said, 'I was hoping you'd tell me.'

I asked some of the crew if they saw anything. No one saw a thing. I dropped the subject right quick. But I figure I saw something, so I decided to use my old contacts. I was an officer in the Air Force in the war, so when I had the chance, I called an old buddy of mine and said, 'Is there anything flying around out here the Air Force is trying out?' He asked me what I was talking about so I told him. He said, 'I'll get back to you.'

I didn't hear anything for a couple of days, then he called me. He said, 'That thing you saw flying. You didn't see it.' I said, 'What the hell do you mean? I *saw* it.' He said, 'You try telling people that and see how quick your studio ends your career.' So I said I'd seen *something*. Was it a plane? He said there were no planes in that region, no helicopters. So then I start thinking, maybe this was some secret Air Force experiment or something. Or maybe it was one of those flying discs. I never got an answer because I didn't pursue it.

I learned quickly you didn't go round saying you'd seen flying saucers. But there were some who saw these things – big name stars. One actor – a big star at Metro – told me he saw one over Nevada one night. It glowed and hovered, danced about, and then shot up into the clouds. I can't tell you who it was. There are others – not many, but a few, and

I can't tell you about those either. I'd rather you didn't print this story.

Well, I didn't print it, not while he was alive. Perhaps if he were alive today he would realize he was in fashionable company and would not mind people knowing he had seen something that seemed to be out of this world. What that something was, he never knew. He told me, 'You could go mad trying to figure out just what it was. But it made me aware just how big the universe is, and that we're pretty arrogant if we think we're the only ones here. Maybe that's why I love our own Earth life so much; our wild life. I figure you've got to have respect for all living things.'

As far as I can make out, *The Streets of Laredo* was filmed in either 1948 or 1949 – it was actually released in 1949 – near the Arizona-New Mexico border, a popular location for westerns. It turns out that Arizona and New Mexico were areas where UFOs were often seen around that time. Roswell, New Mexico, for instance, in 1947.

Among other sightings during that period was one on 7 July 1947, over Phoenix, Arizona, just five days after Roswell. It was seen and photographed by Kenneth Arnold but when his photo appeared in the Arizona *Republic*, the FBI turned up on his doorstep and persuaded him to hand over the photo for official investigation. When he asked for it back a month later, he was told he couldn't have it. Some years later Ground Saucer Watch managed to obtain the picture and concluded that it was not a fake. It was shortly after Arnold's sighting and Roswell that the US Air Force began to look into the possibility of UFOs.

On 24 April 1948, a naval scientist was among a group who saw a white UFO while they were tracking a weather balloon over Arrey in New Mexico. They were positive the object they picked up was not a balloon. Throughout 1948 and 1949 sightings were reported of 'green fireballs' over Los Alamos in New Mexico, as well as over top secret facilities in the American south-west. And it was in 1949 that Project Blue Book was instigated.

11

Hollywood – Land of Cults

Seventy-five million years ago aliens called Thetans invaded the Earth. They were captured and killed by a king called Exenu. The spirits of the Thetans were left to wander the planet and they attached themselves to humans, giving off negative thoughts and bad vibes called 'engrams'. These engrams are the cause of human illness, and need to be exorcized by a special process known as 'clearing'.

If this all sounds too fantastic to believe, there are estimated to be more than eight million people worldwide who have embraced this concept, and among them are Tom Cruise, Nicole Kidman, John Travolta, Mimi Rogers, Priscilla Presley, Lisa Marie Presley, Michael Jackson, Sonny Bono, Kirstie Alley and Karen Black, to name but a famous few.

They are all members of the Church of Scientology, a movement founded by the discoverer of these engrams and their origin, L Ron Hubbard. What would be considered a science-fiction fantasy by most people is accepted as scientific, or religious, fact by Scientologists, all of whom have undergone the mystical rituals that cleanse them of engrams. Now, up to this point in the book, I have refrained from delving into the subject of religion *per se*. Yet it is impossible to avoid the subject altogether since so much of what I have already described is the basis of some religious beliefs. Talking to the departed is a major part of the Spiritualist Church. Reincarnation is a basic principle of Buddhism and Hinduism. Exorcism is a service offered by most Christian churches. And if you are going to talk about the Devil as being the satanic figure who is in direct opposition to all that is good, then you cannot really ignore the concept of God.

Religion and the subject of the supernatural cannot be divided. God and Satan are supernatural beings. But I have refrained from getting into religious arguments, since most religions are at variance with each other over the subjects of ghosts, spirits, UFOs, ESP, hypnotism, astrology and every other aspect of the paranormal. For instance, the Catholic Church and Church of England denounce Spiritualism; Jehovah's Witnesses denounce all other churches as works of the Devil, and Born Again Christians believe that UFOs, hypnotism, ghosts, spirits and other paranormal occurrences are all works of the Devil. Christians believe the Jews got it wrong; the Jews believe they are God's Chosen People and not the Moslems; Hindus and the Buddhists are not in harmony with the Christian Church and vice versa and – well, that is pretty much what the Thirty Years War, the Anglo-Irish and the Israeli-Palestinian troubles have all been about.

But outside all the religious in-fighting something far more sinister is going on. All over the world cults are springing up – the Unification Church (or the Moonies), the Church of Scientology, the Church of this and the Church of that, all claiming to hold the answers to the mysteries of life and death. Some have provided new Messiahs such as David Koresh, whose disciples burned to death with him in Waco in 1993, and the Reverend Jones whose disciples followed him into the jungles of Guyana for a mass suicide pact in the 1970s. There are countless new religions in and around Los Angeles; Hollywood has become the land of cults. They are widely protected by the American constitution and escape official investigation. Yet many of them, the old and the new, represent the darker side of indoctrination, faith and discipleship. It is only a short jump from the word cult to occult.

On the surface, Scientology could appear to be an ideal religion, in that it suits so many top stars – they have found a philosophy that seems to give them more important aims in life than fame and wealth. John Travolta, for instance, hit the heady heights of stardom in the 1970s with *Grease* and *Saturday Night Fever*, then had a long string of flops. He lost his confidence, put on weight and then found Scientology and Kelly Preston. She said of him, 'John has changed because his whole life has changed.' He managed to get back on top again with *Look Who's Talking* and *Look Who's Talking Too*, which, combined, are reputed to have earned him around $15,000,000. In 1991 Kelly got pregnant and they got married in 1991. Then came the enormous success of *Pulp Fiction* and Travolta is right on top again. Yet he said that neither money nor his career is his first concern. 'I know I have to compete, but I don't want to turn it into the driving force in my life. Fatherhood has come late for me [at 40], and I don't want to spoil it.'

When asked by GMTV reporter Fiona Phillips for the secret of a successful marriage, Travolta said, 'Lots of love and care and respect, and probably following a lot of the teachings of Scientology in relationships.'

Travolta said there were so many of these teachings they would fill the *Encyclopaedia Britannica*. Kelly Preston described them as 'the keys to life'.

Here is a picture of a man once plagued by doubts and failure who has now found true happiness through a Church whose teachings may not be in the mainstream but which bring results. It is a picture that would impress anyone. And no doubt Travolta, and all the other stars, have found contentment in Hubbard's strange organization. But his may not be the kind of lifestyle that more ordinary members of that church lead.

That Scientology should be described as a 'church' is in itself a strange concept. Its religious beliefs seem to have no firm foundation on what the rest of us usually accept as being the basis of a church. It certainly rejects Christian doctrine and the Bible and teaches that man is his own saviour. That perhaps is not, in itself, suspect, and may even be an admirable notion. But its method of teaching has been described by its critics as 'mind bending'.

Most if not all religions teach in varying degrees by indoctrination. But when an organization uses techniques of brain washing, or mind bending, then there is something more questionable going on beneath the surface. Any form of mind control (which is what intense indoctrination is, however religious cults like to describe it) has all the elements of the occult. It is as powerful and frightening as any form of the more obviously dark religions.

There is also much controversy over the amount of wealth the Church of Scientology has accumulated and, more particularly, how it has been spent.

No other cult is as star-studded as Scientology. But what makes the likes of Tom Cruise and Lisa Marie Presley willingly give up so much of their personal wealth to be a part of a religion which seems firmly entrenched in the realm of science fiction? Hubbard was, in fact, a science-fiction writer – some say a 'pulp' sci-fi writer – who made his fantastic claims of alien spirits and engrams in his 1950 publication *Dianetics: The Modern Science of Mental Health*. The book taught that human abnormalities and illnesses are the result of engrams which are produced by the unconscious, or 'reactive' mind, which kick into action whenever the conscious, or 'analytical', mind is impeded by pain, drugs or excessive alcohol.

Engrams can begin in the womb, during conception, or in a past life. Individuals who hear words or sounds which are similar to those recorded in the engrams can experience psychosomatic illnesses. Hubbard set up the Hubbard Dianetic Research Foundation in Elizabeth, New Jersey, to teach people how to overcome these engrams. Then in 1952 he moved his base to Phoenix, Arizona, where his activity became known as Scientology. The Church of Scientology was formally created in 1955 and Dianetics became his gospel.

During the past decade the organization has come under increasing investigation and criticism from anti-cult networks and law court judges on both sides of the Atlantic. In June 1984, Judge Paul Breckenbridge of the Superior Court of Los Angeles called Hubbard a 'virtual pathological liar'. After examining evidence, the judge said, 'The documents here reflect his egoism, greed, avarice, lust for power and vindictiveness against persons perceived by him to be disloyal or hostile.' A British judge described Scientology as 'obnoxious, corrupt and dangerous'.

The initiation into Scientology consists of understanding the engrams and overcoming them. This involves an expensive treatment called 'auditing', which costs anywhere between $30 and $14,000 to undergo, during which the new member, or 'aberree,' is put into a semi-hypnotic state and regressed to the point where the subject recalls the origins of the first engrams. This is where the process resembles regression hypnotherapy but may well come closer to the phenomenon known as False Memory Syndrome. This is, in essence, control of the mind.

However, those involved in the cult claim this is not so and that they control their own lives. Priscilla Presley has said that Hubbard's teachings of improving self-knowledge have helped her to enrich and control her own life.

The whole process of auditing remains a secret method but it is thought that something called an 'E-meter' is used, which consists of two tin cans and a piece of string. This E-meter helps to pinpoint the aberree's negative vibrations by measuring electrical resistance. Once the basic engram is discovered, the aberree is in a state of what is termed 'basic' and from that state the remaining engrams can more easily be discovered and disposed of, putting the aberree in a state of 'release,' which means they are free of major neurosis. The next stages are the high states of 'pre-clear' and 'clear', where human intelligence functions at levels well above the average and it is this state that members of the cult seem to aim for.

It is also this 'clear' state that attracts people to Scientology and they seem willing to pay vast amounts of money to gain it. The daughter of Elvis and Priscilla Presley, Lisa Marie, says she owes her life to the church because it rescued her when she was hooked on drugs and alcohol. She married her first husband, Danny Keogh, a faithful follower of Hubbard, in the Scientology Church in Los Angeles in 1988.

When she gave birth to their two children, she had to undergo childbearing in silence, following the strict rules laid down by Hubbard who said that babies are delivered in silence 'to safeguard the sanity of the mother and child'.

In 1993 speculation arose that Lisa Marie would donate much of the fortune left by her father, who was not a Scientologist, to

Hubbard's church. Whether she did, and if so how much, is not known.

When her marriage to Danny Keogh broke down, she remained faithful to the church and, when she began seeing Michael Jackson, she naturally introduced him to it. It is said that he had to undergo the 'auditing' session after about four meetings. Jackson, who was brought up in a family of devout Jehovah's Witnesses, was said by a Scientologist to have 'an open mind, a child-like inquiring mind, and was not prepared to write it off'.

During his meetings Jackson said that he was looking for strength in his ordeal over the child-abuse allegations that plagued him throughout 1994. Apparently he was not subjected to something lesser members have to undergo, allegedly known as 'bull baiting,' in which members sit in groups and endure verbal abuse for hours as a method of learning to control emotions. Hubbard described Scientology as 'the common people's science of life betterment'. However, to achieve life betterment costs money and, in the early 1980s, a number of lawsuits were brought against Hubbard for misuse of funds paid to the movement.

Hubbard died in 1988. He claimed he was 74 trillion years old, but he was born in 1911. It should be remembered that much is published about cults that is often misleading and sometimes downright untrue. But in the case of Scientology, much controversy has arisen over mind-bending methods and the verbal and physical abuse some of its members have allegedly suffered. During the 1970s, a number of Scientologists, including Hubbard's wife, were arrested after attacking anti-cultists.

Yet some of Hollywood's biggest stars have become Scientologists and have seemingly found great happiness. Tom Cruise had originally set out to join the Catholic priesthood and studied at a Franciscan seminary for a year until he decided he was not cut out for the life of a celibate priest. By all accounts, he has always been a spiritual person who puts personal happiness before wealth and fame. He is generally considered to be one of Hollywood's truly nice guys.

It was in 1987, the year he became a superstar in *Top Gun*, that he met and fell for actress Mimi Rogers who is a Scientologist. She introduced him to the teachings of Hubbard and, according to former Scientologist André Tabayoyon, Cruise passed his 'audit', in which he had to reveal his innermost feelings, with flying colours. He also took part in 'bull-baiting' and sat among a group of others to be subjected to verbal abuse and screaming interrogation.

He participated in a 'life orientation course' in which he learned about the aliens who were responsible for the current state of mankind. The aim here was to return Cruise to the state he was in 75 million years before the aliens invaded. According to Tabayoyon, to pass this test Cruise would have had to act out 'psychosis and general madness'.

Cruise married Mimi Rogers but, true to Hollywood form, they divorced in 1990. This was one marriage Scientology's 'keys to life' could not save. That same year he fell in love with Nicole Kidman on the set of *Days of Thunder*. He introduced her to the cult and they were married towards the end of 1990.

It was in 1991 that Cruise publicly admitted to being a Scientologist during a TV interview with Barbara Walters. Until then he had kept it under wraps but, since coming out of the cosmic closet, his efforts to promote aspects of Scientology in his career have not impressed Hollywood studios. For instance, when he was making *Days of Thunder*, the film's producers, Don Simpson and Jerry Bruckheimer, were approached by two leading Scientologists and told, 'Tom would really like the production company to use our sound machine.' This was a hugely expensive sound system developed by Scientologists at an estimated cost of $100,000. Simpson had himself dabbled in Scientology for a while and he took Cruise aside to tell him that Scientology was 'crap'.

When Tom and Nicole were signed to star in *Far and Away*, Tom insisted that Universal use the Scientology sound system. Just why Scientology is involved in creating film and sound technology is not clear, but it appears to have more to do with profit than religion.

After Hubbard died, his work was carried on by David Miscavige. In 1994, André Tabayoyon, a former head of security for the Scientologists, made a deposition through Los Angeles lawyers in which he explained at length what went on behind locked doors. Tom Cruise was named frequently in the deposition. According to Tabayoyon, Cruise was a guest of Hubbard's successor, David Miscavige, at the cult's luxury camp, Gold, at Gilman Hot Springs, California, where some 750 members live and work.

The main building, shaped like a nineteenth-century clipper – hence its name 'The Clipper Ship' – is strictly off limits to the ordinary, non-wealthy members of the cult who work on the camp. But Cruise and other movie stars are said to enjoy five-star treatment, including a luxury restaurant and bar called Camelot, where there is a huge round table like the mythical table of King Arthur. They also have their own apartment cottages.

The camp has a modern cinema, which shows films supplied by the Hollywood cult members. There is also a fully equipped film studio, a golf course, a tennis court and a man-made lake and a yacht. Plus a gym, a sauna and an Olympic-sized swimming pool.

Tabayoyan said that Miscavige befriended Cruise during the latter part of the 1980s. He invited Cruise to the camp and had the film star's chosen apartment rebuilt and improved at a cost of tens of thousands of dollars. Miscavige, said Tabayoyon, was desperate to keep Cruise happy.

Miscavige also had an entire meadow planted with flowers at enormous cost especially for Cruise and Nicole Kidman but the result was so appalling that Miscavige had it ploughed up. A concrete path leading to Cruise's apartment was constructed and he was supplied with his own chef.

Cruise parked his Mercedes, a motor home, and two motorcycles in the garage once used by Hubbard. The cost of all this, said Tabayoyon, came out of funds donated to the church.

By contrast, the ordinary members worked on the camp, in the fields and vegetable gardens and lived on a modest weekly allowance. They were dressed in a uniform of blue shirts and trousers and were rarely allowed outside the camp, which is surrounded by metal fencing, video monitors and radar sensors. They are forbidden to speak to the celebrity guests. Tabayoyon claimed in his deposition that these workers were referred to as the Rehabilitation Project Force and were virtually slave labourers. Miscavige dealt severely with disaffected members, said Tabayoyon, who were held in a punishment camp. Tabayoyon also alleged that Miscavige beat up one man who tried to escape from the base.

There is no evidence or even suggestion that the movie star guests knew anything about any of this. In his sworn statement, Tabayoyon said that 'Miscavige and Cruise have developed a special relationship. One is a world-domineering celebrity. The other is a young, domineering cult leader who seeks to "clear" the world and to rule it according to Scientology beliefs and practices.'

It is said by anti-cultists who have investigated the church that it uses the famous names to woo gullible new disciples. It claims to have more than 8,000,000 members worldwide, including 300,000 in the United Kingdom alone, but anti-cultists, among them established churchmen, say that the overall membership figure is exaggerated.

Cruise has defended the church and his involvement:

> I don't give money away or pay an exorbitant fee. There are no advisers. I believe in taking responsibility for my life. I've based my whole life on whether something works or not. I was diagnosed as dyslexic. There's a Scientology study technology that I applied and I'm not dyslexic now.
>
> We're pretty normal, you know. We do grocery shopping, movies, ice-cream. I do! We go to the movies and we just sign a few autographs, say 'Hi!' get inside, get our popcorn and enjoy the movie. I actually love people. So when they come up and say, 'Hello,' it doesn't offend me. It's actually a nice communication with the people around me.

It is difficult to build an argument that something that brings contentment and happiness to anyone can be at all sinister. But it may well be that the Scientology that Cruise and other big name celebrities experience is not quite the same as that experienced by the ordinary Scientologist. For there is the suggestion that the so-called church is using its star-name members to promote its bizarre doctrines, so that its lesser-known members will spend, spend, spend. But on what?

According to a friend of mine, who was once a Scientologist, the highest state that can be achieved results in levitation. Those trying to achieve this state pay fortunes to do so and, said my friend, no one has yet achieved it.

It is all too easy to say that the ideals of Scientology appeal to people looking for the meaning of life. No cult, or religion, can survive without the charismatic quality of its leader. Reverend Jones had that charisma, so did David Koresh, so did Moses, so did Buddha. So did L Ron Hubbard. These are, whether for good or evil, extraordinary men who are somehow set apart from the rest of us mere mortals. Hitler was another. So was Charles Manson. If he had not been caught and put in prison, there is no knowing what he might have achieved. He may be assumed by some to be just another mass murderer. But he was much more than that. He was the charismatic leader of a cult consisting of people who killed in his name. In 1969, on 8 August, he sent a handful of loyal followers to the Hollywood home of director Roman Polanski and murdered Polanski's pregnant wife, Sharon Tate, and Jay Sebring, Wojtek Frykowski and Abigail Folger.

It was not so much a murder as a ritualistic slaughter (see my *The Hollywood Murder Casebook*). The victims were beaten, stabbed, strangled and mutilated beyond belief. The following night, the same killers went to the home of the La Bianca family, who ran a supermarket chain, and did the same.

The killers, when caught, virtually boasted of their deeds. Susan Atkins gave a detailed account to the grand jury of how she tried to cut Sharon Tate's unborn baby from her womb, even while Tate was still alive. Then Atkins dipped a towel in Tate's blood and wrote the word PIG on the wall.

They all worshipped Manson as their Messiah. They were proud to be a part of his 'Family'. They were caught up in some kind of powerful force which he possessed – he was their Master and he taught them about the occult. He made them base their lives around it. He was a self-made Messiah and he taught them how to enjoy evil.

He had begun his life of crime as a petty thief and was in and out of prison for much of his early life. In MacNeill Island Penitentiary he kept company with drug offenders and read books about satanic worshippers. He began to get ideas about setting himself up as a new Messiah but with Satan as his god.

When he was released in 1967 he went to San Francisco, the heart of the flower-power movement and drug culture, and gave out LSD to teenagers, mainly runaway girls and small-time thieves. They found him to be a magnetic personality. How he had transformed himself into that may have something to do with forces beyond our comprehension. It is certainly true that he fed them so much dope that they reached the point where they believed anything he said and would do anything for him. He was, literally, their saviour.

Members later told how Manson was able to place them in a form of suspended animation. For days on end, they said, they were completely immobile until he chose to release them. Paul Watkins, a dedicated Manson disciple, described Manson's power over them as being like 'mental-thought transference'.

He taught them that evil provided the most sublime joy and that supreme sexual pleasure was to be found in the lust for blood. His disciples considered themselves to be 'Satan's slaves' and he taught them witchcraft and blood-shedding rituals at the Spahn Ranch in the Los Angeles hills.

Manson was never a star of films or music but he wanted to be. He thought he could make it as a musician. Among his friends were Dennis and Brian Wilson of the Beach Boys. According to Bill Scanlon, who produced a TV special for the *Witness* series about Manson's Family, 'Through his Beach Boys friends, Manson infiltrated the sensation-hungry world of Hollywood.

Manson provided them with drugs, he provided them with orgies. There are household names who to this day are fearful that their links with Manson will be made public.' Steve Desper, a music recording engineer, claimed, 'There wasn't much one-on-one sex. It was orgy sex. It was group sex. And it was bisexual sex. Dennis and Charlie and all these girls were in this whole thing together.'

A new theory as to why Manson had Sharon Tate killed is that his targets were actually Wojtek Frykowski and Jay Sebring, two known drug dealers in Hollywood, and that Manson wanted their business. Sebring was known as the Hollywood Candyman because he sold cocaine to Hollywood stars. Frykowski distributed MDS, a forerunner of Ecstasy. According to Bill Scanlon, the investigation of the Tate murders involved a cover-up by the district attorney's office. 'A thorough investigation was going to reveal a lot of unpleasant truths when stones were turned.'

Therefore, the drugs aspect was kept out of the case and the Tate killings were said by the prosecution to have occurred because record producer (and Doris Day's son), Terry Melcher, who actually owned the house which Polanski and Tate rented, was Manson's original target. Melcher had not been seduced by Manson's drug and sex services and had blocked his attempt to become a music star. The prosecution claimed that this was why Manson sent his disciples to kill Melcher but had found Sharon Tate and her friends instead.

None of this, says Scanlon, is true. And if he is correct, then the Los Angeles district attorney's office in 1969 covered up not only a drugs scandal but also a satanic cult.

'The prosecution claimed it was six weeks before the breakthrough came and Manson came under suspicion,' said Scanlon. 'That is simply not true. Just days after the murders he was interviewed by the police. The police had asked Terry [Melcher] if he knew anyone who might want to see him dead. They asked if he knew Charles Manson.' According to Scanlon, Melcher's response to the police was to ask, 'Is this the guy who plays the guitar and all the girls sing in the background?'

Melcher knew who Manson was, and the police were clearly suspicious of Manson.

But when it became obvious that the case would reveal the dirt on a lot of influential Hollywood figures, a cover-up ensued. This resulted in the murders of others in the weeks following Tate's killing. Manson himself decapitated a Hollywood stuntman.

What is known is that when the news of Sharon Tate's murder broke, a lot of Hollywood's most prominent citizens put up the barricades. Jerry Lewis hired bodyguards to watch over him day and night. Frank Sinatra employed a hired gunman and a lot of other movie stars purchased guns and guard dogs.

Sharon Tate was a victim of a satanic ritual. Her killers, Charles Watson, Susan Atkins, Patricia Krenkwinkle and Linda Kasabian, revelled in their blood lust. Just how far this particular branch of the occult had infiltrated Hollywood, and who was involved, remains a mystery.

Whatever Manson originally thought himself to be, it seems he came to think of himself as the Devil's representative on this earth. During his trial he told the jury, 'There are many more coming in the same direction. They are running in the streets and they are coming right at you.'

It was first thought that he was referring to members of his Family who had not been caught but in time it became clear that he was speaking of the 'spirit of evil'. It was a prophecy of human beings driven by satanic forces to commit ritualistic slaughter. Some are concerned that Manson had become possessed by the evil and invisible force that he claimed to promote.

Since then, ritual murders, like the slaying of Tate and her friends, and human offerings by Satanists, have become far more common throughout America. There are those who believe these killings are a fulfilment of Manson's prophecy. And the threat that Manson still poses, even though he is behind bars for the rest of his life, is not lost on Bill Scanlon, 'Just about the only Family member out of jail is Sandra Good. After more than 25 years she is still completely under his evil spell. I have met her several times and I have no doubt that if Manson told her to kill me she would obey without hesitation.'

This, then, is perhaps the darker side of Hollywood. There is nowhere else in the world where so many churches and cults prosper as they do in Los Angeles. How much the influence of these cults is due to the power of the supernatural or to the power of money or just plain charisma is open to debate. It is certainly not all that new, as is seen by the rise of Anton La Vey's Church of Satan in the 1950s.

Of course, had it not been for the death of Jayne Mansfield, La Vey might have never been heard of outside Los Angeles. Almost immediately after Mansfield's death, La Vey openly admitted that he, or his curse, was responsible. He could not be arrested. Murder by curse is not chargeable by Californian law, due to lack of physical evidence. Maybe this was why he claimed credit for the tragedy. Maybe he did have the power of prophecy. He certainly sought publicity. But there is no evidence that his Church of Satan performed ritualistic killings. The only real comparison with Manson is that he was one of Satan's most successful PR men.

Ironically, when Roman Polanski made his Devil film, *Rosemary's Baby*, he hired La Vey as technical adviser. A year after Polanski hired La Vey, Manson had Polanski's wife murdered.

Scientologists may not like the idea of grouping L Ron Hubbard with the likes of Anton La Vey and Charles Manson but these were all men who knew how to control others, many of them influential and famous, and behind these men were, so they claimed, a supernatural power of some kind. Hubbard called it Scientology. La Vey called it Satan. Manson called it the spirit of evil. It has all come a long way from the days when the original Hollywood occultists were satisfied with telling fortunes, reading palms and cards and speaking to the dead.

Afterword

I began writing this book with what I hoped was a clear and open mind. And by and large I think I achieved that. I may have expressed an opinion of my own here and there which displayed a hint of bias and prejudice, but all in all it has been a remarkable journey for me through the paranormal, and the world film stars, Hollywood, theatre and showbusiness generally.

So, here I am, along with you (hoping you are still with me) at the end and I have to admit I may not be quite so inclined to lean so strongly towards opinions I had when I started.

Of course, as this book is a collection of stories I have picked up over the years, many of them given to me first-hand, putting them together has been a case of collating past events and remembering things I had long forgotten. I had forgotten, for instance, the chills I felt when Telly Savalas told me about the stranger who gave him a lift to the gas station and who, it turned out, was dead.

I had forgotten the incredible coldness in the room at Ockwell Manor where one of our gracious kings hanged people. In fact, I had forgotten how, at the time, I had convinced myself that there had to be some normal, rational explanation for the coldness in that room, and in the garden. I had never believed in ghosts, I didn't then, and now... Let's say, I'm not so positive. Although I have never seen a ghost, maybe that coldness I felt really was something out of the ordinary. Something supernatural.

So many people I have spoken to had ghost stories of some kind to tell – Telly Savalas, Kim Novak, Linda Hayden, Michael Bentine, Charlene Tilton and others – and they all believed their experiences. There is no reason not to believe them.

The supernatural or the paranormal – or however you wish to describe experiences that are unexplainable by science – are commonplace for more of us than we might care to admit. ESP is such a common phenomenon that we are often seduced by our fascination and willingness to be overawed by it as a form of entertainment that we ignore, sometimes dismiss, our own personal experiences. TV often offers us 'proof' of psychic phenomena by presenting the likes of Uri Geller on our screens, telling us to watch out for broken clocks that begin to work or spoons that bend in our hands. All we have to do is concentrate on Geller and the objects.

I find it never happens to me. And yet I have discovered that the paranormal as entertainment distances us from what the truth might be. I have found, on just a couple of occasions, that spoons I have used to stir my coffee in the bar of the Quay Theatre in Sudbury, where I was a member of the local Theatre In Education company, have inexplicably ended up bent.

I also used to be able to reach out psychically and touch other people. This I achieved during my twenties. It used to take an incredible amount of concentration to do it, and today I find it too exhausting to manage.

Many professional illusionists claim that they can reproduce the same phenomena without the use of supernatural powers and they insist Geller is just a trickster. Well, maybe he is. I recall a time at the Mayfair apartment of screen writer Jesse Lasky Junior when he told me that Uri Geller had been to visit previously. I asked Jesse if he thought Geller was an authentic psychic. Jesse said, 'All I know is, we had an awful lot of bent spoons throughout the flat.'

I have also had one definite experience of ESP, or premonition. It was a dream that told me what was happening that very night to someone I cared about. On the phone the next day I was able to tell that person what had happened the previous night and we were able to act upon it the following day. So when Vincent Price told me that he saw letters emblazoned in the sky telling him that his friend Tyrone Power had died, when Cliff Robertson told me that he had seen his grandmother in a vision of some kind telling him she was ready to die, when Bette Davis recounted the experience of her mother's vision of her in danger, I am not going to suggest that they imagined it.

A difficult experience to accept without question is NDE – near death experience – but that is because there does seem to be a plausible explanation as to how such hallucinations occur.

However, the fact that people like Elizabeth Taylor, Michael Bentine and Peter Sellers were brought back from death, whatever the medical technicalities might be, is surely an example of miracles, with or without the visions of tunnels and lights. After all, a miracle is how Christians have spent the past two thousand years describing Lazarus being brought back from death.

Now I also have to admit that I have never been convinced that people in this life have spoken to people in the next. Even though I had something of a seance-type experience as a child using an upturned glass – ('Spirit of the glass, are you there?' You know the one.) I was never convinced that it was for real. It told me I was going to be a film producer. I am not a film producer and may never become one because I do not want to develop film producer's ulcers.

But there was no denying that Lynne Frederick was convinced that she had spoken to Peter Sellers after his death. I seem to find myself acquainted with a number of people who are into Spiritualism and it would be arrogant of me to suggest they are all mistaken. I am prepared to be persuaded but I stand by my claim than no one has been told by Marilyn Monroe why she killed herself. If mediums are getting this message, then it does not come from the spirit of Marilyn Monroe.

As a film journalist and an actor, I am only too aware of the superstitious nature of actors, although I tend not to share it. However, I can see how actors develop superstitions very easily, because they do tend to become creatures of habit. When you change out of your ordinary clothes into costume, you usually do it in a certain order, and you invariably feel uneasy if you vary that routine. I like to arrive early if I am doing a play, wander the wings for a while, then get changed, then start going through my lines. This, however, has more to do with the way I 'psyche' myself up in preparation for going on stage than any superstition. Mind you, if my schedule is interrupted, I am not left feeling completely comfortable about it.

I suppose it would be true to say that on the subject of curses, I only ever became anxious about one – the curse of *The Exorcist*.

But that is because when I saw that film, I experienced, for the first time in my life, a pervading sense of evil. Whether this was because it was such a well crafted film which succeeded in producing a certain emotional response from me, or because there was something even vaguely supernatural about it, I cannot tell because, as I have said, I have never seen the film since. But I would suggest that there may be something in the saying, 'Like breeds like'.

That midnight performance of the film at the Warner Cinema in London's Leicester Square was not just another normal media screening. The foyer full of casualties – people who had experienced a range of anxious emotions from vague uneasiness to absolute terror – was not normal.

As for the hype over the other jinxed horror films, such as *The Omen* and *The Amityville Horror*, it may well be that, as with *The Exorcist*, like once more bred like. The trouble is, this all sounds rather irrational, because the rational side of me, which is the stronger, tells me that bad luck or a jinx or however you want to describe a series of unfortunate occurrences is just that – a series of unfortunate occurrences.

That does not necessarily explain what happened to Jayne Mansfield though. Hypothetically, if Anton La Vey knew that Sam Brody had a reputation for driving like a madman, then to predict disaster in a car crash is a good bet. That's a rational explanation. But if there is a force for evil which has its influence on us mere mortals – Satan, the Devil, call it what you will – then it makes it easier to understand the horrors of humanity, whether it be the Nazi death camps, the murders committed by Charles Manson and his disciples, or just the everyday crimes we all fall victim to.

But why certain subjects from history, such as Claudius the Roman emperor and the mutiny on the *Bounty*, should have a curse hanging over them is open to all sorts of speculation. Maybe Caligula or Messalina or Livia really did not like the way Robert Graves depicted them. The same may be true of Captain Bligh. But where the *Superman* jinx comes from is beyond me. It may be that it is nothing but a media invention. It is also true that an awful lot of bad luck has been associated with the fictitious super-hero. Perhaps that's all a jinx is: a word to describe a run of bad luck for which there is no supernatural explanation. It just happens.

As for *Macbeth*, it does seem to be a play which courts bad luck and no one has yet come up with a rational explanation for it. I have to say that I have performed the play dozens of times and only once did I have an accident. Curiously, the sword fight scene, in which I nearly came to grief, is perhaps the one that causes most problems, for Laurence Olivier, for Charlton Heston, for Harold Norman, and even for me. But then, it is a dangerous scene to do if you are going to make it a thrilling action sequence. There are bound to be accidents. Not every performance of *Macbeth* features the sword fight, partly because different directors find different times in history to stage the play, and that often excludes a fight with broadswords.

When all is said and done, I may just give a little more respect to the *Macbeth* curse in future. I have not changed my mind about not wanting to be reincarnated. It all seems thoroughly depressing having to come again. I am not persuaded by the accounts of people reliving past lives. But I am not completely closed to it either. I do recall a TV show during the early 1980s which had as its guest Shirley Maclaine, who was in Britain promoting one of her books and discussing reincarnation at great length. Questions were invited from the live audience as well as from people wishing to phone in from home. The subject of Vikings came up and Maclaine said something about Vikings wearing horned helmets.

A member of the audience mentioned, quite rightly, that Vikings never wore horned helmets. Her reply was, 'Kirk Douglas must have got it wrong then.' She was referring to Kirk's epic film *The Vikings* but, as it happens, he did not get it wrong because none of his Vikings wore horned helmets either. On that day Shirley Maclaine got it wrong. That incident always made me sceptical about the whole notion of past lives. Although I remain willing to be persuaded, I just hope it does not happen to me.

It is curious how certain aspects of the paranormal appear to be more acceptable than others. It is perfectly fine to admit to seeing ghosts, or admitting to an ESP experience, or of being caught up in a curse, or of living in the past. I note, however, a sense of hesitancy about admitting to consulting mediums, although plenty do it. But most of all, the stigma attached to admitting to seeing a UFO does not ease because, despite the growing number of reports, many from civil and military pilots, you are considered to be a bit of out of your mind if you see a UFO, apparently. And, as many, including William Holden, have found out, if you so much as dare to admit you have seen one, you become subject to ridicule and, worse, you can come up against a negative, even threatening, response from military and government agencies. I still do not know if what I saw was a space craft. It was unidentified, it was flying and it was an object. But I never sought an answer at the time and there seems no point in doing so now.

When it comes down to it, I have learned, through writing this book, that despite my own misgivings on certain subjects, there is a whole universe out there I know nothing about. As William Holden said, 'There are more things in heaven and earth – and all that.' And as Fox Mulder asked in the first episode of *The X Files*, 'When convention and science offer us no answers, might we not finally turn to the fantastic as a plausibility?'

Bibliography

Bentine, Michael, *The Door Marked Summer,* Granada Publishing, 1981

Blundell, Nigel, and Roger Boar, *The World's Greatest Ghosts,* Octopus Books, 1983

Brandon, Ruth, *The Life and Many Deaths of Harry Houdini,* Secker & Warburg, 1993

Byrne, James with John Sutton, *Psychic World of James Byrne,* The Aquarian Press, 1993

Callan, Michael Feeney, *Pink Goddess,* W H Allen, 1986

Clarke, Jerome and Marcello Truzzi, *UFO Encounters,* Publication International Ltd (US) 1992

Cohen, Daniel, *The Encyclopaedia of Ghosts,* Guild Publishing, 1984

Fairley, John and Simon Welfare, *Arthur C Clarke's Chronicles of the Strange and Mysterious,* Guild Publishing, 1987

Forbes, Bryan, *A Divided Life,* William Heinemann, 1992

Harbinson, W A *Projekt UFO.* Boxtree, 1995

Harris, John, *Without Trace,* Guild Publishing, 1988

Lazarus, Richard, *Unnatural Causes,* Futura Publications, 1991

Lewis, Roger, *The Life and Death of Peter Sellers,* Random House, 1994

Loren, Sophia, with A E Hotchner, *Sophia, Living and Loving,* Michael Joseph, 1979

Maclaine, Shirley, *It's All In the Playing,* Bantam Press, 1987

Maclaine, Shirley, *Out on a Limb,* Elm Tree Books/Hamish Hamilton, 1983

Rae-Ellis, Vivienne, *True Ghost Stories of Our Time,* Faber & Faber, 1990

Randles, Jenny, *The Paranormal Year 1993,* Robert Hale, 1993

Randles, Jenny and Peter Hough, *Strange But True?* LWT Productions, 1994

Schnabel, Jim, *Dark White*, Hamish Hamilton, 1994

Stokes, Doris, *Innocent Voices In My Ear*, Futura Publications, 1981

Stokes, Doris, *More Voices In My Ear*, Futura Publications, 1983

Strieber, Whitley, *Communion*, Morrow, 1987

Strieber, Whitley, *Transformation*, Morrow, 1988

Swanson, Gloria, *Swanson On Swanson*, Michael Joseph, 1980

Underwood, Peter, *Ghosts and How to See Them*, Anaya Publishers, 1993

Vickers, Hugo, *Vivien Leigh*, Hamish Hamilton, 1988

Wayne, Aissa, with Steve Delsohn, *John Wayne My Father*, Robert Hale, 1991

Wayne, Pilar, *John Wayne, My Life With the Duke*, McGraw-Hill Book Company (US), 1987

Williamson, Linda, *Mediums and Their Work*, Robert Hale, 1990

Articles

'Aliens Stole My Movie', Patrick Goldstein, *Empire*, June 1989

'Daddy Cool', Douglas Thomson, *Sunday Mirror Magazine*, 30 May 1993

'Give Up the Ghost', *Empire*, December 1990

'How Cult Led Jacko up the Aisle', Allan Hall, *Daily Mirror*, 14 July 1994

'It's a Sorrowful Life', Tom Hibbert, *Empire*, November 1992

'I've Lived Before as a Man!', Marilyn T Ross, *Photoplay*, June 1978

'John Lennon in the Spirit World', Bill Harry, *IDOLS*, vol 1 no 2, 1988

'Leader of the Pack', Stephen Rebello, *Empire*, October 1993

'Three Men and a Ghost', *Empire*, November 1990

'Tom's Bizarre Cult Scream-in', Greg Sinclair, *Daily Mirror*, 12 April 1994

Index